SURVIVAL GUIDE FOR COLLEGE GRADUATES

SURVIVAL GUIDE FOR COLLEGE GRADUATES

Fernando I. Soriano, Ph.D.

cognella®
SAN DIEGO

Bassim Hamadeh, CEO and Publisher
Amy Smith, Senior Project Editor
Celeste Paed, Associate Production Editor
Jess Estrella, Senior Graphic Designer
Stephanie Kohl, Licensing Coordinator
Natalie Piccotti, Director of Marketing
Kassie Graves, Senior Vice President of Editorial
Jamie Giganti, Director of Academic Publishing

cognella® ACADEMIC PUBLISHING
3970 Sorrento Valley Blvd., Ste. 500, San Diego, CA 92121

This book is dedicated to my students and to the classes of 2020 and 2021 in the United States and throughout the world who are living through historical events rarely experienced by students in the past.

BRIEF TABLE OF CONTENTS

DETAILED TABLE OF CONTENTS

PREFACE

T he COVID-19 pandemic hit us in California around mid-March of 2020 when all instructors at my university were told all classes would be immediately converted to remote teaching. I distinctly remember the moment the university announced that we were no longer having in-person class sessions. I was with my students in class. I reminded them of a lecture I gave early in the semester when I shared a story about the challenges that students faced during the Great Recession of 2007–2009 and about the practical things that they could do to increase their competitiveness during challenging economic times. Even before the pandemic crisis came, economists had already been talking about signs in the economy of an impending recession. With so many businesses being asked to immediately close, I knew that the health crisis was going to turn into a combined health and economic crisis that would affect the career and job opportunities for college graduates.

It was during this time of having remote sessions with my students that the idea of writing an economic "survival manual" for graduating college students came to mind. It was specifically during a particular Zoom information session that I had with my students in the 2020 Spring semester that I mentioned the possibility of writing what I hoped would be a helpful document that would guide them through the crisis that would likely be marked by high unemployment and few employment options. The goal of the class I was teaching at the time was to prepare graduating seniors for what they would do following graduation. In addition, the class required them to do a minimum of 90 hours of fieldwork at a health or human services organization. Through lectures and presentations, the class also exposed students to the various available career options given their degree in human development, which is an interdisciplinary social science degree.

At the time, I told them I would share the manual in an upcoming Zoom session. As it was to be a manual, I thought I would quickly prepare a short written guide offering a list of suggestions and advice that would help them get through the impending economic crisis. But then, when writing the outline of the topics I thought I could or should write about, the task became more onerous given how much I could say that I felt would be helpful. Needless to say, with such a short time before the end of the Spring semester, I did what I could, and out of that effort came what was at that time an 80-page manual. Since then, I reached out to colleagues who suggested that I publish the manual as a book in order to broaden the audience to all graduating seniors, regardless of field, and even to those who are unemployed. Kassie Graves was my previous managing editor for the last book I wrote on needs assessments. Through our work together, I came to regard her as a trusted and dear friend. She had since moved to Cognella Publishing as an editor. I sent her the manuscript to get her advice on its publication, not thinking of Cognella as a possible publisher for it. To my pleasant surprise she told me Cognella was indeed appropriate given its series of books covering the various personal and academic concerns facing college students. Thankfully, she supported publishing the book through Cognella.

This manual, now a book, is indeed broader in scope and can be profitably used by all graduating seniors, regardless of field. It is also relevant and helpful to those looking to either find new employment, enhance their career, or help in competing for jobs by guiding them in knowing the value of their degree and experience. While this book is no longer focused on those from my field of human development, you will find that I use that field as an example to discuss issues and advice that cuts across most fields. At present, due to the pandemic crisis, the economy is only now beginning to open. Many businesses, such as restaurants, movie theatres, and gyms, have permanently gone out of business. We do not know what the economy will look like after it fully opens, but it is likely to be challenging for new graduates and for those laid off or unemployed. This book is sent forth as an offering from one professor who cares a lot for his students in the hope that they and others reading the book will benefit from the insights and advice it contains.

Even if you do not agree with the advice given, I hope it will stir your thinking and will lead to better planning and action. I have emphasized to my students the importance of proofing their writing before sending it out to others so as to avoid criticism or low expectations from the person receiving the written material. That includes assignments, emails, or cover letters. Due to the shortness of time to prepare the initial document, it unfortunately did not serve as a good model for them to follow. Unlike the early "manual," I trust that this book will not have as many such errors.

This book was written from the heart and based on knowledge and experience gained over the years and with the concern for each of my student's well-being foremost in my mind. You will notice that most of the chapters are short. Written as a manual to help make quick decisions, I did not want readers to have to read extensively to get to helpful advice and suggestions. I also wanted to include reflective questions posed to the reader that helps them personalize the information and cause them to think of its application in their lives. At the end of the book, there is space for the reader to note insights, more long term plans, and decisions. That is what makes this book a survival manual!

I want to express my gratitude to my students who, through Zoom sessions, informed me of their fears and challenges and provided me with information that helped me identify issues and information I needed to cover in this book. I offer a special thank you to Kassie Graves, editor and vice president of Cognella, who encouraged me throughout this process, from the time I presented the concept to the finished draft. She is not only an amazing professional with so much wisdom and experience that she so generously shared with me but I also consider her a dear friend whose personal encouragement made this work so much more enjoyable. Last, but certainly not least, I thank my wonderful wife Sissy who always offered me encouragement. You were so patient when I was not around during the many early mornings and late evenings I spent working on this book. I also thank my two boys, Anthony and Fernando, who were always so encouraging and who cheered me on throughout.

PART I

INTRODUCTION TO THIS GUIDE

CHAPTER 1

INTRODUCTION

It is May 8, 2020, and in two weeks my students are going to graduate with their classes done and with their degree requirements completed. SARS-CoV-2, which can lead to the COVID-19 disease, has caused the world to defend itself by imposing restrictions in the movement of populations. Most states and cities have mandated stay-at-home orders or the wearing of masks. On Friday, March 13, 2020 I had my last in-person class right before the university told us we were not to come back because they were closing to avoid spreading the very contagious coronavirus. Fast forward to May 9th when I am having my final Zoom discussion session with my students. It has now been two months of state-mandated stay-at-home isolation for all in California. Like other instructors, I converted my regular in-person courses to remote online courses. I could have continued to mandate synchronous meeting as a class through Zoom, but I felt that neither I nor my students could handle the mandated meetings since we were all trying to adjust to this major change in our academic and personal lives.

The courses I have taught lately have been field experience courses, which give students the opportunity to develop experience, skills, training, and knowledge by volunteering for mainly nonprofit organizations and schools. Before the public health mandated isolation, my students had gained about half of the required 90 hours of field experience. Now they had to stop and do self-study that would be substituted for the remainder of the 90 hours of fieldwork they were not able to do with an organization because of the restrictions. The self-study allowed students to gain an understanding of the skills, knowledge, training, and experience that they would have acquired in the field but would now learn through readings and by watching educational films and videos.

During our Zoom class discussion sessions that I had on a weekly basis, I noticed the deep concern that students had regarding their futures. Over 50% of the students at our university are first-generation college students, meaning that they are the first in their families to attain a college degree.

Most students had been working, often full time, while also taking a full load of classes. Many have now been laid off from their jobs because of the pandemic. Many have been employed in service jobs, such as food servers, grocery store cashiers, and retail clerks, to name a few. Their anxiety, stress, and depression was evident during our remote sessions. Most admitted to struggling with their mental health during this time of uncertainty and upheaval. The last time such a sudden economic downturn happened was during the Great Recession of 2007–2009. Early in the semester, before the pandemic crisis hit, I shared with students how during the Great Recession jobs were extremely scarce and unemployment was high. Professionals with bachelor's and master's, and even doctorate, degrees fought for opportunities for even nonpaid volunteer or field experience opportunities just to get a foot in the door with organizations or businesses with the hope of eventually getting a paid job.

Of course, historically, we have always had recessions or economic downturns, but never had I witnessed such scarcity of jobs and such a sense of futility among so many professionals in so many fields as during the Great Recession. I remember voting as a faculty member to have my pay cut through furloughs to keep people employed at the university. I shared with my students how, back then, as department chair, I went out to meet with employers to see what we in our department could do to prepare our graduating seniors to best compete for the few available jobs. To my surprise, employers that I spoke with in the human and social services area were encouraging. For example, the county social work division manager I met with cried on my shoulder, telling me how desperate her division was to have social workers who knew how to work with clients that were educationally, culturally, and socially diverse and how they wished they could hire professionals who had good interpersonal relationship and communication skills and who worked well with others. I was told that if I could prepare students to have such people skills, they would likely hire them immediately, even with the current, serious economic downturn.

Some predict that the current pandemic crisis is likely to cause another serious economic downturn that will likely rival that of the Great Recession since the whole world is being affected, causing economies to stop or at least slow down significantly. On the other hand, at the time of printing, so far the economy is doing relatively well probably because of unprecedented federal assistance, which has its limits. Either way, this book intends to help students, like my graduating seniors, and anyone wishing to know their worth in the job market having their degree. My intention is to help the reader be appreciative of their education, training, and job experience. I hope to prepare the reader for what may or may not be a hostile economic environment marked by a scarcity of jobs and career opportunities.

I include information that I believe will help the reader to best prepare and compete successfully for the positions that they wish for and that are available. As this is a book written in the form of a manual, students or readers are encouraged to go through each chapter and to check off each topic covered to be sure that they have considered the relevance of each to them personally.

The information covered in this manual or book comes from years of experience and observations based on what I have witnessed. I have seen what happens during economic downturns and have learned what helps students succeed in spite of an economic downturn. At the end of each chapter, there are questions and topics posed to help the reader consider how the topics covered in each chapter relate to their own situation. I hope that the reader will use the space available at the end of each chapter to write down notes and reactions to these topics, making this a personalized manual.

With the exception of Chapter 2, the rest of the chapters are grouped into three sections. The first section, "What You Need to Know and Do to Succeed," tries to pass on a deeper understanding of the meaning of your degree, the different names for it, how it is used, and how it is regarded by employers. In this first section I help the reader increase their understanding of their worth in the job market and help them know the skill set they have gained and possess, along with increasing the personal understanding of yourself that leads you to value yourself and have that reflected in an application or job interview. The second section, "Taking Action and Making Decisions," contains chapters that provide information that pushes the reader to understand the condition of the economy and job market so that decisions are made in the context of your personal economic need and situation. These chapters help the reader consider the various viable options available, which can help with job market impasses. The final section, "Personal Considerations," deals with the personal issues and challenges they are likely to encounter, such as stress, anxiety, depression, substance use and abuse, and interpersonal conflict. Chapters toward the end provide advice on protecting yourself from negative outcomes by developing positive habits that lead to a more peaceful and encouraging environment, even during challenging economic times.

MY OWN NOTES AND REFLECTIONS ON CHAPTER 1

Questions and activities to consider, besides your own notes.

To what extent are you excited and interested in having a manual that gives you advice and prompts you to plan ahead?

What are your expectations for this manual? Make a list of the concerns and issues that this survival manual can help you with.

_____

_____

_____

_____

_____

_____

_____

_____

_____

_____

_____

_____

_____

_____

_____

_____

_____

_____

_____

_____

_____

_____

CHAPTER 2

IDENTIFYING AN ECONOMIC DOWNTURN AND ITS SEVERITY

C urrently, the world is focused on slowing down the spread of the coronavirus and on providing medical assistance to those who have been infected with it and are developing COVID-19 health complications. Discussions have been increasing in regard to the impact the disease has had on commerce and on the economy. We already know that millions of Americans have applied for unemployment assistance due to the pandemic. The national unemployment rate reached a peak of 14.7% in April 2020 compared to the prepandemic rate of 3.5% in February of the same year.[1] But how do you know whether to get worried about the economy or if it is going to go through a major recession? There are three indicators that you should watch out for that are tied to a recession:

Amount of Spending: The more abrupt and deep the retraction in public and private spending, the bigger the recession.

Rising Unemployment: The second thing to look for is the unemployment rate and its rise. Again, the more rapid the increase in unemployment rates, the more likely you will see negative effects on the economy leading to a recession.

Negative Hiring Levels: The third indicator is the level of hiring taking place or *not* taking place in broad and varied sectors of the economy. The more quickly a reduction and change in hiring rates across diverse sectors, the more likely you will be experiencing the effects of a recession.

Inflation and Deflation

There is a fourth indicator that I did not list, because it is not always present during a recession but is nevertheless a strong precursor or indicator of an impending recession. It is when the cost of living or housing hits peaks to levels that are unsustainable with current income levels, as was seen during the Great Recession of 2007–2009, or when there are unexpected and precipitous drops in such costs. Right before the Great Recession hit, people were going through an unrealistic frenzy, with people commonly engaging in bidding wars with others trying to buy properties, thinking that the risk of taking out a large loan would lead to immediate profits due to unsustainable, ongoing price increases that in theory could be realized in just a few months. The banks were in on this lending and buying game of people taking out loans for properties that were overpriced. People and businesses gambled, thinking they would be able to sell their acquired properties and secure a substantial profit before the economy tanked. Unfortunately, it was only a matter of time, and when the economy did tank, it led to what we now call the Great Recession because it rivaled the Great Depression of the 1930s in its widespread impact. Housing prices then started their downward dive, which led to many people having banks repossess their high-priced homes. Many lost their jobs and their homes because they could no longer afford their mortgages. Even rent prices were not sustainable. Numerous families were without homes or jobs, with little prospect of finding employment. As mentioned earlier, as a department chair and instructor, I felt bad for my students because of the lack of hiring taking place and worried about their future career outlook. It took several years for the country to recover from that recession.

To this day, students who graduated during that time recall the deep worry that they had and how their career courses were altered. Graduating seniors at that time often ended up taking jobs in the private sector, such as in insurance, sales, or retail. Over time some rose up the ranks and now find it difficult to revert back to their focus on gaining health, human, or social services positions because they would have to start anew in an area they never got entry-level experience in as a graduate with their bachelor's degree. If you were one of those affected this way and you are not happy in the field you ended up going into, it is not too late to change, but you will need to follow the instructions given in this book to be able to relate your work experience to the job sector you originally wanted to get into, be it in business, science, engineering, health or human services.

Sector-Specific Depressions

I do want to make a distinction between a recession and other problems, such as occupational retractions, that can adversely impact one sector of the economy. For example, the need for teachers at the primary or secondary level has vacillated greatly depending on the number of teachers that are or are not retiring and also due to declining birthrates. Also, occupations like nursing sometimes evolve in the health care system where new health technicians and medical assistants are increasingly taking over past duties of nurses, and nurses are increasingly being placed in supervisory roles overseeing many of those who are in emerging occupations. When thinking about choosing a professional career or job, make sure you read about the demand for those careers and jobs—not that you need to decide for or against going into these, but doing so will let you know what the demand is for that job or career. That information will give you an idea of the extent to which you will compete with others in that field.

Follow Your Passion

You will always hear me say that if you are totally committed and passionate about a particular professional career, you will be successful in it even if it is not in demand. Why? Because you have the ability to focus on, specialize in and learn more about that particular field. You are able to look someone in the eyes, like of a job interviewer, and convey that sense of fit and knowledge that someone who only wants a job but lacks the passion cannot demonstrate. Once in the job, that same passion and focus on the field will also allow you to go up the ranks since your employer will see that excitement that is so needed in any organization or business. That same passion will also allow you to adapt when the occupations undergo changes—something that all those in any field or career will need to be prepared for. Finally, that passion will give you the motivation to learn and exhibit those vital interpersonal and communication skills so necessary to secure employment.

Note

1. Statista. (2021). *Monthly unemployment rate in the United States from December 2019 to December 2020.* https://www.statista.com/statistics/273909/seasonally-adjusted-monthly-unemployment-rate-in-the-us/

MY OWN NOTES AND REFLECTIONS ON CHAPTER 2

Questions and activities to consider, besides your own notes.

What are the signs of an economic downturn in my community?

How would you describe your community in terms of being worried or hopeful about the economy or job prospects?

What are the attitudes of those around me toward the economy?

Briefly describe the economic and employment situation in your city or region. Point out fields experiencing the most job losses and areas of job growth to consider as opportunities.

Describe any passion you have for a career or occupation and your willingness to stick with it no matter what.

_____

_____

_____

_____

_____

_____

_____

_____

_____

_____

_____

_____

_____

_____

_____

_____

_____

_____

_____

PART II

WHAT YOU NEED TO KNOW AND DO TO SUCCEED

CHAPTER 3

KNOW YOUR DEGREE

The Worth of Your Major

Many university students are first-generation students or at least second-generation students who are the first or second in their families to get a four-year college degree. My parents did not have a college education or even finish high school. Consequently, like many of the readers, I did not have parents who could guide me on what college is all about and of its value. My father wanted each of his seven children to become medical doctors only because he hated bosses and he thought that doctors were those fortunate few who did not have to have bosses and always earned a lot of money. My sister was the closest to going into medicine by becoming a nurse, earning her Associate of Science degree in nursing. The rest of us rebelled and became anything else but a medical doctor. The point is that many students do not have mentors who have adequate knowledge about degrees and their value in the economy. The sad fact is that even upon graduating from college, many seniors often lack the knowledge of the degree that they worked so hard to get, let alone know its worth.

What Is a Bachelor's Degree?

Let us start with considering what a bachelor's degree *is*. It is a college degree that about one third of those 18 years or older in the United States have but that the vast majority, or about two thirds, do not have.[1] Without saying anything else, please ponder those statistics. *You having a degree— whether it's a BA or BS—that fact sets you apart from most of your adult peers in the United States in a significant way.* That means that you professionally stand out! Employers know that and will value it. Know your worth. Graduating seniors first need to know that their degree is unique and is worth a lot. Tattoo that fact in your mind, please. I say that because there is a growing tendency for undergraduates to feel that bachelor degrees are now considered high school degrees something further from the truth.

According to the U.S. Bureau of Labor Statistics, in 2019 adults over 25 who had a bachelor's degree earned an average of $27,664 more per year compared to those who only had a high school education.[2] These are important facts because how you value what you have will determine how confident you will feel when you apply for a job or for entry into a graduate program. If you feel like, "Ah, everyone has a BA. It is now like a high school education!" then you will convey that sentiment to yourself and, equally importantly, to others.

Use the Effect of the Emperor's New Clothes Concept

Have you heard of the emperor's new clothes concept? It plays out every day in the field of clothing fashion. *The Emperor's New Clothes* is a 1800s folk tale that was written by Hans Christian Andersen about a king who was swindled by two conniving thieves who convinced the king that their royal clothing was amazingly beautiful but was invisible to those who were dumb and incompetent. Convinced by the swindlers, the king paraded through his kingdom to show off his new clothes. Afraid of what the soldiers would do, the public feigned admiration for the new clothes as the king paraded until a small child audibly whispered to his mother that the king was naked, thereby revealing the truth to all, including the king. A good modern example of this can be seen in the way that celebrities pay thousands of dollars for clothing that is made of materials that may or may not be unique but are certainly worth just a fraction of the money paid for the apparel once it is put together by famous designers. And though they may look awkward in their unflattering, avant-garde attire, they come across as confident and assertive, making audiences think that the clothing is great. People may criticize their attire or point out facts, like the child in Andersen's story, but amazingly, most people play the social game and are convinced by those that convey that confidence. So if self-assurance can convince people that they are somehow special even when they have glaring imperfections, just imagine how much more important it is for you to value your degree, which, in fact, did pass on to you a significant amount of knowledge of the world and of others, along with practical skills. The point is that you need to have surety and confidence in the degree you worked so hard to attain.

However, just like celebrities who tout their special clothing made by high-end fashion designers, such as Calvin Klein or Gucci, you too need to tout your degree and know its worth. First, let us start with the field that your degree represents. Because many BA degrees do not train you for specific occupations or careers but for an array of them, students can feel like they just have a basic degree. They forget to fully understand the importance of their specific major that they chose and the skills, knowledge, training, and experience that the classes they took for the major afforded them. Let me take human development, the major in my department, as an example. It is an interdisciplinary major that exposes students to classes that provide an understanding of the social, psychological, biological, and cultural context of human beings across their life span, from birth to death. Most students taking classes for their major just take them to get that piece of paper that shows they have a four-year degree. When they apply for a job or graduate program, they are sometimes stumped when they are asked "What did your major prepare you for?" or "What is Human Development?" or, "What is ..." (fill in the blank with your specific degree, be it engineering, psychology, sociology, biology, computer science, etc.).

Know Your Degree's Worth Through Classes Taken

Of course, some people may recognize a field like psychology as one that trains people to be therapists or clinicians. But without further graduate training beyond an undergraduate degree, you cannot be licensed to do actual therapy. So what does the undergraduate degree in psychology prepare you for? When asked after finding it challenging to find employment, students with this degree may think to themselves, "Dang, maybe my degree was worthless! My degree and major was just a bunch of required classes on a lot of topics—many that I liked and a few that I didn't! But what was it good for since I find it difficult to get a job?!" Some may become the proverbial deer in the headlights when asked to explain their degree, including by parents or family members—frozen, unable to explain well the significance and application of their degree because they did not fully understand or appreciate the worth of their degree even while earning it.

Let me assure you that your undergraduate education was not just a mass grouping of classes and requirements. Any undergraduate degree gained in any accredited school is a well-planned program of study, and once you recognize its planning and purpose, you will have a deeper sense of satisfaction in having finished your degree. If you are getting a BA degree in human development, for example, you can be proud of how the grouping of required classes in the field have provided you with a solid understanding of the multidisciplinary and interdisciplinary theories used to understand human beings from social, psychological, biological, and cultural contexts across the lifespan. If you are completing or already completed your BA or BS degree in psychology, your required classes likely taught you to understand human beings from a psychological perspective; you learned to read, understand, and critique research literature, and you know the dominant theories for understanding the attitudes, thinking (cognition), emotions, and behavior of human beings. If you have received your BA degree in sociology, the courses you took from the major provided you with a solid understanding of the sociological theories used for understanding human beings within social, cultural, and societal contexts. You also learned about the quantitative and qualitative methods used in the field.

The point is that all undergraduate degrees, whether they are in the social sciences, humanities, business, or the sciences, give students a solid foundation of knowledge that is vital for understanding our world, its people, history, methods of study, and critical thinking and have introduced you to various theoretical frameworks that explain what you see, know, and use in making decisions. If you are going into graduate school, graduate programs want to know that you indeed learned to use critical thinking skills for understanding and using knowledge coming from various perspectives for making conclusions and decisions. They will want to know you learned about methods used to develop valid and reliable knowledge.

Do a Detailed Analysis of the Courses Taken

If you look at your transcript, the list of courses taken will tell you what you know. You will see that the knowledge conveyed by your degree has incredible value in our economy and in the job market. Bring to mind specific courses you took and consider what they mean to employers and to graduate programs in terms of the skills, knowledge, training, and experience you have as a result of them. When you took a class on statistics and research methods, for example, you were learning to understand how knowledge is derived, what society uses to make significant decisions, and the challenges we face when we want to know the truth about any question we have. Statistics and methods classes allow you to look behind the knowledge curtain to better judge the value of research findings and information. As a result, when you hear that the medication Remdesivir is being introduced to address SARS-CoV-2 to help those with COVID-19, you are able to see that the sample size used to date in the United States has been just 1,063 persons and that while the effect on those who took the drug was on the more positive side compared to those who did not take the drug, the effect is modest and may not be reflective of the broader population that perhaps was not represented in the original sample. Those taking the drug recovered in an average of 11 days compared to 15 days for those taking a placebo. You learn that statistical significance is different from practical significance. Do the increased risks and secondary effects of a powerful drug outweigh the four days you save in recuperating from the disease? You at least learn to ask such questions based on your statistics and methods classes.

If you took an applied course in your major, like psychological testing from psychology, families and intimate relationships from sociology, or effective counseling interventions across the lifespan from human development, you gained a lot of practical knowledge that has value to employers, graduate programs, and even to you personally. From the psychology course, you learned how the field of psychology diagnoses individuals with psychological conditions or pathologies. If you took the sociology course, you learned about the importance of families and the impact of having intimate relationships that will allow us to either thrive or be adversely affected by them. If you took the human development course, you learned about effective interdisciplinary methods of counseling that consider the developmental stages and cultures. Many students who took this class might not realize its value in pointing to the importance of effective communication and listening—something that employers commonly feel is lacking in their employees. Knowing and conveying knowledge and possession of such skills gained from such classes can likely be the deciding factor in being selected for a job or entry into a graduate program. When going through your transcript, write out at least one main piece of knowledge, training, skill, or experience you gained from each class that you think any employer or graduate program would want to know you have gained.

Understand the Philosophy Regarding American Undergraduate Education

Liberal Arts Degree

What is your degree, anyway? This may seem like a funny, if not a perplexing, question to pose, but it is an important one to consider. Unfortunately, not too many students know their degree well, beyond knowing topics covered by it. Allow me to explain that a bit further. Most BA degrees are called *liberal arts degrees*. That means that in the United States, our pedagogical philosophy is one where we feel as a society that exposing students to a breadth of knowledge coming from various fields produces better, more well-rounded students who are able to continually learn and adapt to the needs of society and of employers. This is different from other countries, such as those in Europe, that instead believe that college-level education should prepare you for specific jobs or occupations. Undergraduate degrees, as practical as their courses may be, do not train you for a specific job or career. They may prepare you for fields but not for specific occupations. For example, if you got a degree in computer science, you likely took courses that led to you having knowledge and skills in areas like programming or operating systems. However, unlike degree programs in other countries, even science and technology undergraduate degrees in the United States still require students to take classes from various fields that include the humanities, social sciences, math, and sciences as lower division or general education classes. Taking these lower division courses is how you meet what is called your general education requirements. As part of your general education requirements, you commonly take classes in areas such as science, math, language, English, social sciences, and history.

Of course, when you major in a field, you take courses that represent the field. That is, when you take classes in your major, you are expected to learn the breadth of the field you are majoring in. You typically do not develop a specialty. Required courses in a major represent a sampling of topics representing the field. For example, if you majored in fields like psychology or sociology, you may have been required to take classes that covered various subfields. In psychology, you may have taken personality, psychopathology, social psychology, experimental psychology, and so on. If you majored in sociology, you may have taken classes like law and society, inequality, or families and intimate relationships. If you majored in some interdisciplinary field, like human development, you probably had to take courses on interdisciplinary theories used in the field and classes that surveyed the breadth of the interdisciplinary field, such as social services, child and youth development, adult development, and gerontology. The point is that you were not expected to develop a specialty in any one subfield. If you were excited about a particular subfield, or area within a field, you can continue your education and specialize in just that field. When I got my doctorate in psychology, I chose to specialize in social-personality psychology. Only then did I mainly focus most graduate classes on that specialty.

Knowing that you took classes that represented various areas within any field that you majored in is important for you to know so you can use that knowledge to your advantage when you sell yourself to an employer or graduate program. Most of the time students just have a list of required courses that they check off without standing back to consider the importance and relevance of each class to the job they are seeking or graduate program they are pursuing. As a side issue, you need to consider the skills you learned when taking classes from various fields that included learning how to do literature searches for those papers on diverse topics. Through these literature searches, you learned to identify and retrieve knowledge, to critically assess it, and incorporate it in a particular themed paper assignment. Those skills are incredibly valuable for employers to have resident in their workforce.

Social Science and Behavioral Science Degrees

Beyond knowing that your degree is a liberal arts degree, you should know that degrees in psychology, sociology, or human development are all social science degrees. A *social science degree* is one what provides students information coming out of the social sciences. Social science includes human development, psychology, anthropology, sociology, and specialized fields like ethnic and women's studies. When employers advertise for someone with a social science degree, you will be able to say that you have such a degree. That is important since you will find very few jobs that will ask for a degree or specialty in a particular field. Few employers will say they want someone with a psychology or sociology degree. They may use them as examples of social science degrees, but they will typically not require such specific degrees.

The other thing you will see employers looking for are those who have a behavioral science degree. Those with a degree in human development, psychology, sociology, anthropology, and other social science-based degrees can claim to have a behavioral science degree as well. According to the Encyclopedia Britannica, a *behavioral science degree* is a degree in "any of various disciplines dealing with the subject of human actions, usually including the fields of sociology, social and cultural anthropology, psychology, and *behavioral* [emphasis added] aspects of biology, economics, geography, law, psychiatry, and political science."[3] Clearly, many of the classes you took in your social science field dealt with human action; therefore, your degree can also be considered a behavioral science degree, and as such, you can share with employers and prospective graduate programs how you learned about human action and behavior.

STEM Degrees

STEM is an acronym for the fields of science, technology, engineering, and mathematics, which actually covers other specific fields, including biology and physics, for example. I am sure you have heard a lot in the media about how we need to increase the number of our students majoring in STEM fields. The reason for this is that future developments in health, science, and technology require students who have a basic knowledge of math and science. As with social science fields and majors, those who majored in any of the STEM fields did not develop a specialty in any of the subfields but rather received a sampling of the basic areas encompassing the field. For example, if you majored in mathematics, you likely had to take various algebra and calculus courses and learned about probability and number theory. Besides giving you a good foundation of the fields of algebra and calculus in particular, they provided you with the type of knowledge that employers need to plan for and develop products or, at the very least, plan for inventories and deliveries of those products.

In essence, you gained basic skills and knowledge that when combined with experience and further on-the-job training, will be valuable. As with social science degrees, the key is to understand the worth of your degree and to understand the various applications of the knowledge you gained from the classes you took that represented various subfields. It is also important that you value the liberal studies philosophy of your education that also required you to take courses outside of your major, which included basic skills in oral and written communication, critical thinking, arts and humanities, social sciences, and lifelong learning. Do not make the mistake of ignoring the value of these other "general education" courses that employers and graduate programs value tremendously. Having professionals who know how to read, write, defend their critical thinking, and understand the world and people around them is vital.

Just like with other social science degrees, you can also talk about how your degree in biology, computer science, engineering, or math are science degrees. You can say "I have a science degree." As such, you can qualify for almost any job that requires a knowledge of science. The only caveat is that there are some science fields that are more specific in their training and can narrow the application of your degree. For example, if you major in engineering, you will need to choose one of several engineering fields. It would be difficult for you to use your degree in aerospace engineering to apply for a structural engineering position since each engineering field trains you in understanding specific areas or applications.

Arts Versus Science-Based Degrees

A Bachelor of Arts, or BA, degree means that you took mainly liberal arts classes and that the classes you took, particularly at the upper-division level, were not focused on math and science. Some employers and graduate programs require that students graduate with a major that required the completion of a minimum number of science or math classes. In fields like psychology, you will find some departments will offer choices of either BA or BS degrees. The BS degree will require students to take more science and research courses related to psychology, including intermediate statistics and advanced methodology. Students with a science-based degree will claim to know more about research and statistics related to the field, along with other courses that are taught from quantitative perspectives. Most employers and graduate programs who want students with science or research backgrounds may prefer one with a B.S. However, BA awarded students can also emphasize to such employers or graduate programs that the classes that they took, like math, statistics, methodology, or applied research, all provided them with a solid understanding of the use of numbers and statistics considered important by many employers. The same can be said when talking about MA or MS degrees, although they are a higher level. MS degrees always suggest greater training and skills in the use of numbers and quantitative methods.

The Humanities

Finally, students need to know what the humanities are and how they relate to the classes they took for their degree. According to Wikipedia, *the humanities* are academic disciplines that study human culture. ... The human-ities use methods that are primarily critical, or speculative, and have a significant historical element—as distinguished from the mainly empirical approaches of the natural sciences. The humanities include the study of ancient and modern languages, literature, philosophy, history, archeology, human geography, law, politics, religion, and art.[4]

Some of the areas encompassed by the humanities include fields that are sometimes thought of as part of the social sciences, which include anthropology, area studies, communication studies, classical studies, law, and linguistics. The humanities teach us how people, primarily in the past, created or understood the world around them.

Fields that typically fall under the umbrella of humanities include literature, history, modern languages, philosophy, religion, visual and performing arts, music, and theatre. Anthropology can also be considered as being part of the humanities since it teaches us how people have created their world, and how they in turn are created by it. Some of the courses and electives you took for your degree taught you about people and their experiences in the world around them. So you should know that you have exposure to the humanities through your classes and through the elective humanities classes you took. As such, if you really liked a particular class from the humanities and you feel the employer or graduate program would appreciate it, you can share how your BA degree also helped you to understand human beings, how they created or shaped or have historically reacted to the world around them. You would then share how a particular class or classes you took provided you with that knowledge and experience.

The point of this chapter is to prompt you to understand the importance of your degree and the specific courses you took that have value in and of themselves to you, future employers, and graduate programs. Now when you hear terms like liberal studies, social science, and sciences, you have a more in-depth understanding of your degree and what it represents. You know that all degrees, whether coming from the humanities, social sciences, or the sciences, required you to learn about the world around you and its people and histories. You also learned that all majors required you to demonstrate good written and oral communication and critical thinking skills. The key is to know the value and worth of your degree and to be able to convey that sense of worth to future employers or graduate programs.

Notes

1. U.S. Census Bureau. (2017). *Highest educational levels reached by adults in the U.S. since 1940* (Release No: CB17-51).

2. TED: The Economics Daily. (2019). *Median weekly earnings $606 for high school dropouts, $1,559 for advanced degree holders.* Bureau of Labor Statistics, U.S. Department of Labor. https://www.bls.gov/opub/ted/2019/median-weekly-earnings-606-for-high-school-dropouts-1559-for-advanced-degree-holders.htm
3. Encyclopedia Britannica. (n.d.). Behavioral Science. In *Encyclopedia Britannica.* https://www.britannica.com/science/behavioral-science
4. Humanities. (2021). In *Wikipedia.* Retrieved January, 17, 2021 at 16:54 (UTC), from https://en.wikipedia.org/wiki/Humanities

MY OWN NOTES AND REFLECTIONS ON CHAPTER 3

Questions and activities to consider, besides your own notes.

How well do you feel you know your degree and its worth?

What information mentioned in the chapter did you not know that you want to make sure to retain?

List the classes you have taken that you feel have provided you with the most marketable skills, knowledge, and training. Next to each class, list those things you gained from the classes.

_____

_____

_____

_____

_____

_____

_____

_____

_____

_____

_____

_____

_____

_____

_____

_____

_____

_____

_____

CHAPTER 4

WHAT EMPLOYERS WANT IN EMPLOYEES

There are common skills and abilities that all employers want their employees to possess. This includes skills in communication, interpersonal relationship, critical thinking, and problem solving. Let us look at these and other skills more closely. Having good communication skills sounds easy, but it is not as easy as you think to possess or develop them. Of course, when we speak of communication we are including both oral and written communication. Let us start with written communication skills since they seem to be in great demand in all fields—science, social science, education, or humanities.

Importance of Writing Proficiency

If you meet with employers hiring BA-level educated individuals, you will find that they are often clamoring for individuals who have good writing and oral communication skills. Unfortunately, many college-educated individuals fail to put importance on learning to write correctly (i.e., avoiding grammatical or spelling errors). If there is one piece of advice to retain from this book, it is to proof your writing when applying for jobs or graduate programs. Do not rely on your own proofing; have others look over the drafts of your applications or emails inquiring about jobs. I have told my students that I, Mr. PhD, commonly make grammatical and spelling errors when drafting the simplest of messages, be it emails or written instructions to students. I always find errors in what I write when I read it twice and even find errors when I read it a third time! Sometimes it is because of missing or incorrect words that I corrected in my mind as I was writing but didn't actually correct them on the page. In this book, you may even find some errors not caught by me or the editors. So please pay attention to details when you write, but also reread what you write to catch the errors you will undoubtedly make.

The other thing for many of us to acknowledge is that perhaps we never really learned to write well in the first place. For whatever reason, we never learned well the skill of communicating in writing. It could have been due to deficient teachers or due to the lack of importance we put on developing or enhancing our writing skills. Writing is, in fact, a skill, and as such, we need training to develop it properly and to enhance it. Even if you are graduating, decide that you will enhance and improve your writing skills. Consider taking a creative writing class at a community college. Take a class that teaches you writing but does it in a fun way. The other way we learn how to write is to read books and to pay attention to effective communication through writing. Whatever you do, please put importance on your writing, on reviewing what you write, and improving it.

Oral Communication

This one sounds easier than written communication, but actually, it is just as hard if not harder since oral communication involves words and nonverbal communication. Back in the latter part of the 1960s, Albert Mehrabian, a communication researcher, along with other colleagues, conducted studies that have been used to emphasize the importance of nonverbal communication, which according to them accounts for 93% of our communication.[1,2] Another way of saying this is that only 7% of our communication are the actual words we say. The other large percentage includes the vocal tone or inflections and our body movement, including our posture; facial expressions; movement of our head, hands, and arms; eye contact; and our physical proximity to those we are talking to. I remember seeing a TED talk where the speaker was saying that they studied the most viewed TED talk videos, and the one thing that came up as significant was the hand and arm movements. Presentations where speakers used their hands and arms more to express themselves had the most viewers.[3]

In our minds, we hear ourselves and have a sense of what we are saying, and in general, we do a decent job of communicating. However, now that you are entering the professional realm with your degree, you need to improve your oral communication. Record yourself and pay attention to the intonation you use. Are you monotone when you talk, making yourself sound boring, or do you have voice inflection that keeps the attention of your listener? Do you maintain eye contact when you speak to people, or do you tend to look away and cause your listener to lose their attention? What is your body posture when you talk to professionals? Is your body posture straight or maybe even leaning forward and conveying that you are sure of yourself and of what you are saying, or are you slouched with slightly drooping shoulders, which can convey that you are not sure of what you are saying or of yourself? Part of good oral communication is also being attentive to your listener and to their verbal and nonverbal cues.

My wife knows that I am a terrible listener. I justify to myself thinking it is because I multitask a lot. It is easy for me to have my mind veer out when people are talking to me, to think of some noncentral thought, perhaps based on a word being mentioned by a speaker. Let me give you an example:

> **Speaker:** I think, like Freud, that we need to learn more about people's early childhood experiences to really understand them!

> **Listener (me—internally reacting to *some* of what the speaker is saying and thinking to myself):** Hey, I wonder if Freud said some-things about communication in his writings. I should look into that. Maybe Professor Romig knows about that. After all, she studied Freud. Oh, and I should call and see how she is doing with the pandemic. She is probably busy, because she is a nursing professor ...

The speaker sees me listening, but I am probably lost in thought on other topics. The point is that some of us are very poor listeners and are easily distracted. We need to be trained to listen since it does not come naturally to us. If you are like me, you need to seek training, which starts with you first acknowledging that need. We need to learn to always bridle our thinking to really hear what is being said and patiently wait for the speaker to finish their thoughts fully. One way I bridle my wavering mind and listen attentively is by practicing reflective listening skills, where I force myself to repeat what the listener said to verify my comprehension. Practice reflective listening to improve or enhance your listening skills! "So you are saying that early childhood experiences are important in shaping people as adults?" You summarize what the speaker is saying emphasizing the point they are wanting to make.

Interpersonal Relationship Skills

I remember talking to the county's child welfare division once during the Great Recession when no one was hiring but rather were laying off workers. That was a horribly painful time for me as a professor, worrying about my students finding a job or even of being able to get into a graduate program. To my surprise, the people in charge of hiring within county child welfare told me that they were still able to hire social workers. Even with the number of people looking for jobs and the numerous applicants that they had for social worker jobs, they were not able to find the right applicants who had the necessary skills. I remember a hiring supervisor telling me that even with the high unemployment rate in the region at that time, they would hire my students immediately if they demonstrated the ability to relate well with others. She said it was challenging to oversee social workers who clashed with clients and even with other social workers because they did not know how to interact interpersonally. Think of those you have met in retail or in restaurants who failed to look you in the eye or wait to hear you out versus those who demonstrated true interest in not just listening to you but also relating to you interpersonally.

But what are good interpersonal relationship skills? According to an article on the subject, the interpersonal skills that are most valued in the workplace include:

- **Active listening:** you are engaged with the speaker, encouraging communication by asking questions or by paying attention to their nonverbal cues.
- **Communication:** the simple ability to speak with most people and be effective in expressing yourself.
- **Courteous and Professional:** being sensitive to others and treating them kindly and professionally, minimizing subjective evaluation or preconceived notions.
- **Dependable:** you can be counted on and see tasks through to their completion.
- **Empathy:** the ability to place yourself in the shoes of others and to understand where they are coming from. It does not mean you accept the views of others but that you can understand why they feel or perceive things as they do.
- **Flexibility:** the ability to adapt and to change as needed.
- **Leadership:** while not everyone needs to be a leader of departments or programs, they should reflect leadership qualities, such as the ability to listen to others, empathize, and have patience. If you have these skills, you will likely be asked to take on leadership roles.
- **Motivation:** employers go crazy over employees who demonstrate high levels of motivation. They do so for two main reasons. First, when being around a motivated person, you get motivated yourself. Second, it encourages those around them and makes the work environment a positive one, even in the face of challenges.
- **Teamwork:** this is probably one of the most mentioned traits that employers are looking for—the ability to work well with others and to work as part of a team, feeling comfortable giving directions and accepting directions. It includes the ability to treat all as equals and to give and receive feedback.

    Learning Attitude: people with this trait or skill are willing to learn. It probably goes with flexibility, but it is the willingness to learn new procedures, methods, and ideas. This is not on the list in the article, but I feel strongly that this needs to be mentioned as a part of having good interpersonal relationship skills.[4]

You can see from the aforementioned list that having good interpersonal relationship and communication skills means that you understand how multidimensional it is and how you need to keep each dimension in mind when demonstrating interpersonal relationship skills with others.

Critical Thinking Skills

Professors always talk about critical thinking skills and their importance. On the surface, it sounds important. Critical? Well, it must be important to be critical! Thinking? Obviously, it's important to be good thinkers in college! When presented with the combination, critical thinking, we say, "Yes, of course—they both naturally go together!" But, on average, do we *really* know what critical thinking skills are? My sense is that many of us do not. And if you do not know the concept well, how are you to have this skill, develop it, or demonstrate it? I like this definition of *critical thinking*: "The objective analysis and evaluation of an issue in order to form a judgement."[5] In other words, it is you setting aside your assumptions, biases, and wishes on any subject matter or decision at hand and opening your mind completely to consider the objective data or information at hand and committing to using that objective information to make a wise and informed judgement or decision—all based on facts, to the extent they are available.

    At universities, we are sometimes a bit hypocritical at times. We want you to think critically, but on the other hand, we like to tell you what is "fact" and "truth" and teach you its value. We do that when we test you through "objective" exams. It is not that we are purposeful hypocritical, but we are so short on time with so many in our classes and so much knowledge to go through in a semester. As a result, we end up short-changing debates on what is fact or what is truth by not taking the time to thoroughly review all the evidence. If and when you attend graduate school, you will see that critical thinking is much more the expectation, demand, and practice. I remember when I started my doctoral program and we as students had to take courses called *proseminars*. These were courses made up of about no more than ten students—all at the doctoral level. We were given an amazing amount of readings to do each week, usually published books and/or journal articles. We met weekly, and I hardly had any lectures from professors but rather the professors seemed to have the role of facilitating discussion and of questioning. The professor might say, "From his book, what can we learn about Harry Triandi's thinking about what is important or not important for understanding human behavior and motivation in the context of culture and society? What are your own views?" The first time this happened to me, I was the proverbial deer in front of headlights. However, I quickly learned that the other students in the class and I needed to not only be able to gain information but to identify it and be able to convey it to others.

It was up to us to make sense of publications and to learn to either see their value or argue for or against them and their conclusions using objective facts and data. You could not simply say, "Oh, I really liked it!" and get away with such a simple assessment. You needed to break data or information down into its different parts and decide whether or not to use it in future discussions or studies. That is critical thinking: when we learn to listen objectively to the voices of people and valid publications that present objective information or data, where we are able to listen to sources of information to understand differing views as much as possible, utilize facts that are available to make sense of the information, to learn to accept and use the information or not, to be swayed by differing arguments or not. In practical terms, for you as college graduates, you need to develop the skill of collecting facts when questions or problems arise and to utilize the facts to make decisions, give opinions, or find solutions to problems. Critical thinking means that you will never be quick to judge right away but will listen first; you will not make decisions before collecting objective data to use.

The funny thing is that employers and even some graduate programs sometimes fall into the trap of thinking that they know it all or think they are following the practice of utilizing critical thinking by simply taking the word of others they subjectively select as "those who know truth" without being more objective by listening to various views. You will always be an asset to organizations, businesses, or graduate programs when you follow the practice of listening, collecting objective data, and utilizing it to argue one view or another by always being willing to have others present alternative views based on different data sources that may supplant your own analysis. If you are truly open to critical thinking, you will always be willing to say to those presenting convincing objective data, "Looks like you are right and I'm wrong."

Having a Learning Attitude and Information Resources

The discussion regarding critical thinking goes along with the need for graduates to always have or to develop an attitude of learning from others, be they people you know, such as mentors and supervisors, or people you have never met who publish books or articles. To have a learning attitude means that you will have an ability to listen and not always be quick to make judgements or to talk. It requires empathy towards another person's views. It also means that you will supplement the listening of others with readings to compare views espoused with published views. With the internet and social media, there is an ocean of written information on all kinds of topics. If you want to learn about the health hazards of caffeine, you can do a Google search and get all kinds of websites that let you know how dangerous caffeine is to our health. Reading them, you will probably stop drinking coffee, fearful of the negative impact it has on your body, including the increased risk of cancer. However, if you do another Google search on the health benefits of caffeine, you will see how beneficial it is to our health and how it is said to even prevent certain types of cancers. So, what is the truth, seeing as the information is often contradictory online? The truth is probably in-between both views, but you will not know what to do unless you do your own search for more objective information—probably not relying on Google searches but rather on scholarly literature searches that identify peer-reviewed journal articles.

Web Search Advice for Finding More Factual, Noncommercial Information

One suggestion for doing searches for more objective information is to tell Google to delimit the search sources to more objective sources of information. Using the example of finding the dangers or benefits of caffeine, you can tell Google to search for only government, education, or nonprofit organization sources. For example, when doing a Google search, type the topic you wish to search information on, such as "dangers of caffeine," and then type, "Site:.gov," "Site:.org," or "Site:.edu." Either of these will then give you only search outcomes that come from the government (.gov), from nonprofit organizations (.org), or from educational institutions (.edu). It avoids the (.com) businesses that normally want to advertise.

Peer-Reviewed Publications

Having a learning attitude also means knowing when to give credence to information and when not to. Remember to pay attention to publications that are peer reviewed compared to those that are not. Peer-reviewed publications are those that went through a vetting process where facts and conclusions are checked by knowledgeable professionals. This book, for example, was sent out as an early draft to peers for their feedback on its content. Many websites containing information on the web are normally not peer reviewed. This is not to say that information coming from .com's is erroneous. It is just that you do not know for sure. To help you put faith in information on the web, you need to see the credentials of the person or group producing the information. Always verify the information and conclusions found on the web by going through peer-reviewed publications obtained from city, university, or college libraries.

Consider going through review articles and chapters that present a literature review on any subject matter. A good source of information on almost any field and subject matter covered in a field is the Annual Review series or volumes on various fields relevant to the social sciences or sciences. For example, I routinely look for reviews on youth violence, my specialty area, in the *Annual Review of Psychology* or in the *Annual Review of Public Health*. In the sciences, there are also the annual reviews of various areas of biology, be it plant biology or developmental biology, to name a couple science sources. Here is the Wikipedia link that lists out all the annual reviews for various fields (https://en.wikipedia.org/wiki/Annual_ Reviews_). Use these and other reviews to get up-to-date information on almost any subject area.

Regarding knowledge on careers and jobs, everyone should go through the *Occupational Outlook Handbook* published online by the U.S. Bureau of Labor Statistics, which is part of the U.S. Department of Labor. Go through it and you will find information on various careers, qualifications for them, and pay ranges, including for those in your region. It will also give you the future outlook for many careers.

Having a learning attitude is critical in today's ever-changing world. The technological changes taking place make it important that we know how to embrace new technology instead of being bothered by it. Your learning attitude, coupled with the right information sources, will help you to use your critical thinking skills that are so vitally important for you as you move forward in your selected profession, whichever you end up choosing.

Notes

1. Mehrabian, A., & Weiner, M. (1967). Decoding of inconsistent communications. *Journal of Personality and Social Psychology, 6,* 109–114.
2. Mehrabian, A., & Ferris, S. (1967). Inference of attitudes from nonverbal communication in two channels. *Journal of Consulting Psychology, 31,* 248–252.
3. TEDx Talks. (2017, June 27). *Vanessa Van Edwards: You are contagious.* TED Conferences. https://www.youtube.com/watch?v=cef35Fk7YD8
4. Dayton, D. (2019). The difference between interpersonal relations and skills. *Chron.* https://work.chron.com/difference-between-interpersonal-relations-skills-18645.html
5. Oxford University Press. (n.d.). Critical thinking. In *Lexico.com dictionary.* https://www.lexico.com/en/definition/critical_thinking

MY OWN NOTES AND REFLECTIONS ON CHAPTER 4

What are those traits mentioned in this chapter that you feel you have, and which do you feel you do not have? Next to your career goal or career options, list those traits that you feel you should have in order to be successful in them. Indicate where you stand in having those job traits. Develop a realistic and specific plan for developing, improving, or excelling in any marketable trait. List any other traits you think are important that were not mentioned.

_____

_____

_____

_____

_____

_____

_____

_____

_____

_____

_____

_____

_____

_____

_____

_____

_____

_____

_____

_____

_____

CHAPTER 5

WHAT EMPLOYERS *SHOULD* WANT IN EMPLOYEES

In the previous chapter, I presented information on the skills and knowledge employers are actively looking for in their employees. In this chapter, we will discuss what all employers *should* be looking for in employees in terms of skills, knowledge, and understanding in regard to people. I also discuss knowledge that you gained from your classes that employers would be impressed that you have, along with knowledge you would do well to gain through your own self-study that would make you an impressive applicant.

Importance of Understanding Human Beings

Because of our country's liberal arts philosophy of education, all students obtaining a BA or BS in the United States have to take some classes in the social sciences. For example, regardless of your major, you may have taken Psychology 101 or Sociology 101 to fulfill a social science general education requirement. If you majored in a social science field, like psychology, human development, family studies, sociology, or anthropology, you took more than just a few social science courses. Through any of these courses you would have gained knowledge that helps you understand human beings, be it their behaviors, motivations, developmental stages, gender or cultural differences, and so on. Regardless of whether you are going into a science, business, social science, or any other field, all employers value those who are able to understand and work well with others.

More specifically, all good employees or prospective employees need to know something about the psychological, social, cultural, and biological context of human beings. Why? Because we work with human beings! Our success in careers and in our personal life is tied to our understanding of and ability to relate to others. We need to pay attention to courses that have taught us about the psychological, social, biological, and cultural context of human beings, across the life span. If courses did not teach these contexts of human beings, you need to read about them and become familiar with them.

Psychological Context

The *psychological context* includes gaining an understanding of our cognitive thought processes—how we think, reason, and make decisions that lead us to our emotional state and behavior. For example, positive psychology has received a lot of attention due to its relevance to and application in the workplace. Founded by Martin Seligman, positive psychology emphasizes the control we have over our happiness, positivity, and well-being. In a journal article entitled "Positive Psychology in the Workplace," Larry Froman focuses on the role that hope, joy, gratitude, interest, inspiration, and pride play in allowing us to be happy in life and in the workplace.[1] He considers hope to be critical for lifting up the human spirit when facing challenges, such as those that took place during the 2007–2009 recession and those that are likely taking place now at the time of the book's publication.

As mentioned in earlier chapters, the Great Recession caused many college graduates to feel hopeless because finding a job or entering a graduate program was so challenging at that time. Froman, quoting from Federickson, suggests that hope is the key to feeling control over your life. Hope is the "belief that things can change. No matter how awful or uncertain they are at the moment, things can turn out better. Possibilities exist. Hope sustains you. It keeps you from collapsing into despair. It motivates you to tap into your own capabilities and inventiveness to turn things around. It inspires you to plan for a better future."[2] As with hope, we have control over our thinking that allows us to consider things we are grateful for, such as our health or the relationships we have. We derive joy from feeling grateful for those things that are most meaningful to us.

Positive psychology complements one of the most successful therapeutic modalities currently used, called Cognitive Behavioral Therapy (CBT), where the focus is on the therapist helping clients to identify and change destructive or disturbing thought patterns that have a negative impact on their emotions and behavior. Essentially, clients are guided by a therapist to develop a positive self-appraisal and future outlook through processes that allow them to focus on putting negative experiences or thoughts in perspective. Strategies are offered, such as journaling, role-playing, and relaxation techniques like meditation and mindfulness. Positive psychology and CBT both emphasize the power that individuals have in developing a positive outlook on life even if they face current challenges or past traumatic experiences that haunt them. Social or psychological classes that you may have taken perhaps mentioned or even taught you about positive psychology or CBT. If not, read up on it. The knowledge you gain will help you to deal with self-doubt and with other practical challenges that come with a failing economy.

Social Context

The social context of human beings is often intertwined with the psychological context, yet the social context by itself needs to be given special consideration. People, like our parents, for example, have a tremendous impact on our enduring, life-long self-esteem and self-image. Parents and close family members or caretakers provided us with the initial basis for the understanding of ourselves. However, those around us are critical for supporting or refuting a positive or negative self-concept of ourselves. If we are in the midst of a serious recession or national crisis, like a pandemic, those around us will often be the deciding factor on whether we panic or stay calm. Our social surroundings will influence the type of outlook we have toward life and how we present ourselves to others who will decide whether we will get a job or gain entry into a graduate program. The successful entrepreneur and motivational speaker Jim Rohn first proposed the idea that you are the average of the five people you spend the most time with. You need to surround yourself with positive people who encourage you and not with those who criticize you.

Here are some possible characteristics of those who can be toxic to you versus those who can have a positive influence on you.

Toxic Influences	Positive Influences
Jokes at your expense.	Counters your own self-criticism.
Makes fun of you.	Defends you when others criticize you.
Reminds you of your mistakes.	Reminds you of your positive traits.
Conveys doubt about your judgment and thinking.	Makes positive remarks about you.
Hardly ever makes eye contact with you.	Conveys trust in your judgement and thinking.
Does not seem to listen to you when you speak.	Supports you when you say you can succeed.
Cuts you off when you speak.	Does not laugh at you or use you in jokes.
Laughs when you are talking.	Always attentive when you speak.
Will often take sides with those who criticize you.	Makes eye contact with you during conversations.
Avoids you when you are down.	
Avoids helping you when you need it.	
Easily tells you to give up on your efforts.	

(continued)

Toxic Influences	Positive Influences
• Does not provide helpful suggestions for confronting serious challenges you face. • Isolates you from others.	• Wants to spend time with you when you are down. • Always willing to help you when you need it. • Contributes helpful ideas to deal with challenges you face. • Encourages you or helps you find others who can be helpful to you.

Find people who can have a positive influence on you, especially when you are stressed or face challenges in finding a job or when trying to gain entry into a graduate program.

I have presented things you should do to help you be surrounded by those who can be of support to you. However, the point of this chapter is to point out things that employers should want in employees. Having employees surrounded by those who uplift and encourage them is fine. But what employers really want is to know that you know how to work with others successfully. They want to know that you can engage in critical thinking with others, contribute to finding solutions, and work as a team to accomplish necessary tasks. Getting along with others will invariably lead to more effective interpersonal communication and lessen misunderstandings, because you feel comfortable checking on your understanding with others. What employers should also want is to hire those who have the necessary social and interpersonal communication and relationship skills necessary to establish a positive organizational culture that is able to handle challenges and find creative and effective solutions to them. Taking care of yourself by being surrounded by encouraging peers is something you can tout and discuss during a job interview or in your application.

Biological Context

In contemporary research, we are learning about the importance of our biology and genetics and how they affect our behavior, emotions, and thinking process, or cognition. It is estimated that no more than 50% of our individual differences are caused by genetics.[3] The other 50% is our environment, which includes what we do to ourselves and what is in our environment. What we eat, for example, determines the balance in our biology. We are learning that our gut biome contains 500 to 1,000 separate species of bacteria that can be placed in two categories, called phyla: firmicutes and bacteriodetes.[4] According to an article in *Psychology*

Today, studies have shown that gut bacteria and your gut biome can influence your anxiety, stress, and depression levels.[5] Most undergraduate students take biology classes that teach them about the connection between the body and the mind.

A focus on biology also includes the impact of our diet on our emotions. More and more we are learning about how the sugars we ingest affect our body and our mind. We have all heard about the evils of eating too many carbohydrates. The reason why carbs get a bad rap is because they are essentially sugars. Carbs are made up of saccharides that are molecules that convert into complex molecules in the form of starch, fiber, and simple sugars that become metabolized into glucose. The simple sugars that convert to glucose are made of carbon, hydrogen, and oxygen. The point is that glucose, either in the form of simple sugars or starch carbohydrates that our bodies convert to glucose, which affects our energy levels and mood. When eating them in a meal, they will immediately increase our energy level as they are quickly introduced in our blood stream, but then our system sends insulin to counter or reduce the glucose and that causes us to immediately reduce our energy level and mood, making us feel irritated or tired as we become hypoglycemic. Beyond the impact on our mood swings, it puts us at risk for Type 2 diabetes or tooth decay.[6]

I remember growing up with my father who was diabetic. He actually ate pretty healthy most of the time. Maybe he ate a bit too much, but he still ate balanced meals, always including some fruit as dessert. However, he loved cakes and Mexican pastries that were not available in the rural part of California we lived in. But when we had a birthday celebration, and my mom made a cake—boy, he went crazy for it. I remember my mom telling him not to eat too much cake because he was diabetic. My dad became deaf during those times and he would eat his piece of cake with an ear-to-ear smile on his face. Almost without exception, soon thereafter he became irritable and feisty, arguing with everyone. Thank God we lived on a ranch with lots of space and animals that we ran out to until his sugar levels normalized! Regardless of whether you are diabetic or not, eating too many sugars and carbs will affect you and your mood. During times of stress caused by a recession, we need to be mindful of the foods we eat.

Many of the biology classes you have taken have taught these facts. Employers need to have employees who understand these biological influences. In some ways, this is why a lot of employers are expanding their Employee Assistance Programs, called EAPs, to include wellness programs that help employees stay healthy, because they are becoming aware of how workplace productivity and job satisfaction is increased when employees are healthy.[7] Besides nutrition, employers are focusing on encouraging employees to get fit and exercise since research is clear on the psychological and physical benefits of doing exercise—something you need to remember from your biology and even some psychology classes that covered this topic. Taking care of your health and body is something you can also mention during an interview (if you are, in fact, taking care of yourself in these areas), which will make you stand out as an applicant.

Cultural and Gender Context

I am covering this last, but it is certainly not the least important characteristic that employers should want in their employees: an understanding of people and their cultural and gender diversity. Most undergraduate students and social science majors have taken classes that help the students understand the important role of culture, age, and gender when considering almost any outcome, be it health, income, education, mental health, or housing. Almost every social science class incorporates some discussion on the role of culture, development, and gender regardless of the specific course topic. You do not need to be an ethnic or cultural minority to be sensitized to or made aware of the cultural discrimination that cultural minorities face daily due to stereotypes (conscious or unconscious) tied to their culture, physique, or skin color.

Some students have taken anthropology classes out of interest. Unfortunately, some anthropology courses we decide to take cover the history of aboriginal people that is interesting to consider, but in the end, we sometimes fail to see the relevance of those tribal groups to our modern world. These classes, while enlightening, end up giving us this distorted view of others who are different from us as being less relevant or intelligent than we who live in a modern and urban world. The courses that benefit us and that help us better understand those different from us are those that show how we *all* are an important part of social and cultural diversity.

I remember going to Europe for the first time and seeing people who all looked like mainstream Americans physically, but culturally, they were very different—beyond their language. When asking for directions, I remember feeling uncomfortable with how close they all seemed to get to me, almost talking face to face. Physical distance norms seemed to be very different. They say that as Americans, we typically like to stay about three feet from those we are talking to, whereas Europeans are more likely to stand two feet from us or less. If I ask students in my class to describe their cultures, Hispanic or African American students seem to have things to point out that are unique to the cultural groups they belong to. However, those who are third or more generation Caucasians normally find it difficult to describe their culture. They typically will say, "I'm American!" But if I probe further and ask them about their roots, they will typically say that their parents have historical roots in some European country or countries like Italy, England, and Germany or are mixed.

Probing further, they will realize that the food they eat and some of the traditions they have as a family have roots in their parents' families of origin.

The fact is that we all have diverse cultures within us. As Americans, we may share many things in common with others since over time we do form our own set of cultural practices and traditions. However, it is important to accept that we all have to understand others who may be culturally different from us. That means that we need to pay attention to the differences and read more about them as well. Our nation is blessed with being a country of immigrants that is among the most culturally diverse in the world. Everyone, except for Native Americans, have roots with people who came from another part of the world to settle here in the United States. Employers need employees who take the time to understand and accept the cultural diversity that is resident in their service population and also among their peers. Some of the classes you took in school discussed cultural diversity, and perhaps we were not ready to listen and to retain that knowledge, but during a recession, this is the type of knowledge that employers need and will make applicants for programs and jobs the most competitive. Even if employers do not put that in their job descriptions, they will be glad to know you have knowledge and, hopefully, experience working successfully with diverse populations.

In the same way, most human development courses consider the important role that gender plays in social, cultural, and economic discrimination. Such sensitivities and knowledge help you become a better employee and eventual supervisor who is sensitive to disparate treatment of individuals by society. As graduating seniors, you need to know the value of the education and learning you have acquired and have it clearly understood and ready for you to discuss when facing an interview panel that asks you the question "Why should we hire you or why are you so special compared to other applicants?" If you took ethnic studies or gender studies classes, make it a point to mention the knowledge gained through these courses in such interviews. Make sure that you make it real and not superficial. By making it real, I mean that you should apply the importance of the knowledge gained to the work to be accomplished at a worksite or to the populations the organization is serving. The worst thing to do is to say that you are culturally sensitive or competent when you do not even know what it means and how it is anyone gets to be culturally competent or sensitive towards any social or cultural group or gender.

If you are not an ethnic minority or do not belong to a gender that experiences discrimination, you likely belong to another group that is discriminated against by society that can allow you to empathize with others. For first-generation college graduates, they usually come from a family and possibly a community that is impoverished. I remember as a seven-year-old, the stress of dealing with only two sets of cloths to wear to school because my parents did not earn much money. In order to cope, I remember wearing turtle neck "dickies" in cold months that were false turtle neck shirts that you would wear under shirts. The problem with my two dickies (one red and one blue) was that my little neck was too thin as a young child in second and third grade, so I had to used safety pins in the back of the turtle necks to keep the turtle neck tight. That type of experience was not so much traumatic, but it also set me up for discrimination by those teachers who would look down on me and my family for being poor. In fact, to this day, I feel that a long-term substitute teacher put me back a grade just because I came from a poor family. So many of our students who are first-generation students have all experienced similar discrimination because they were poor or because they came from broken homes with only one parent in the household who was barely making ends meet. Use any negative classification and negative experiences you have experienced to help empathize with various groups and to bring about insights that can help you in your application for a job or graduate program.

Societal Issues and Challenges

The other things that students have learned through their classes deal with *social justice issues* and challenges that populations face in society. For example, if you took a course like Youth and Society, Youth Violence, Child Development, or Family Violence, you understand the challenges that youth and families face living with scarce resources or in broken homes and yet somehow survive these often-horrific challenges and become productive adults thanks to their personality and/or individuals who believe in them, trusting that they can overcome adversities. If you took courses in subjects like health disparities, increasingly being offered in colleges, you have learned about the challenges that health and resource disparities cause for populations across the life span. Employers commonly work with individuals who have such social, educational, economic, and cultural treatment disparities. As students who took education or social science courses or graduated from social science fields, you understand factors that can lead to healing and overcoming serious challenges, including understanding evidence-based programs and services that are vital. The important thing is to consider the broader societal issues and events that shape us.

I, for example, have begun to understand the important role that our economy has on delinquency or violence rates among youth. If parents are unemployed or have to work at two full-time jobs to make ends meet, that leaves youth unsupervised, which increases the likelihood of getting involved in behavior that puts them at risk for negative outcomes, including not being able to focus on their education. I remember when I conducted a study on youth when I was a professor at Stanford and learned that many middle school students felt pressured into joining gangs just to have protection from being jumped walking home from school. I saw how the economy and income challenges of families have direct consequences on the rates of violence and delinquency in the area. It became clear that to address the problem of delinquency, we need to see the broader societal pressures that struggling families have to bear.

Knowing about these higher order societal problems is important when looking for a job that is in the social sciences or even when manufacturing products that require sufficient family income. You may come up with a wonderful product that is helpful to families, but if families are struggling economically, even wonderful products will have challenging markets. The point is to become aware of broader societal issues facing the populations or markets of interest. Even mentioning your awareness of these higher order societal challenges will set you apart from other applicants.

Notes

1. Froman, L. (2010). Positive psychology in the workplace. *Journal of Adult Development, 17,* 59–69.
2. Fredrickson, B. L. (2009). *Positivity: Groundbreaking research reveals how to embrace the hidden strength of positive emotions, overcome negativity, and thrive.* Crown Publishers/Random House.
3. Anthony, A. (2018, September 29). So is it nature not nurture after all? *The Observer* (blog hosted by The Guardian). https://www.theguardian.com/science/2018/sep/29/so-is-it-nature-not-nurture-after-all-genetics-robert-plomin-polygenic-testing#:~:text=The%20key%20to%20personality%20traits,from%20personality%20to%20mental%20abilities.
4. Human Microbiome. (2020). In *Wikipedia.* Last modified version on May, 2, 2020. https://en.wikipedia.org/wiki/Human_microbiome
5. Azab, M. (2019, August 7). Gut bacteria can influence your mood, thoughts, and brain. *Psychology Today.* https://www.psychologytoday.com/us/blog/neuroscience-in-everyday-life/201908/gut-bacteria-can-influence-your-mood-thoughts-and-brain
6. French, A. (2018, December 6). What kind of carbs is cane sugar? *SFGATE.* https://healthyeating.sfgate.com/kind-carbs-cane-sugar-8955.html
7. Litwack, S. (2016, November 16). *Employee assistance programs and wellness.* Best in Corporate Health. https://bestincorporatehealth.com/employee-assistance-programs-wellness

MY OWN NOTES AND REFLECTIONS ON CHAPTER 5

Questions and activities to consider, besides your own notes.

To what extent do you have a good grasp of the various stages of human development?

Identify one age group you are likely to work with in your career and prepare yourself for developing expertise in it.

What social or health problems did you learn about through your classes that are important to keep in mind when working in a health or human services setting? Focus on one social or health problem that you are likely to need knowledge on in the likely places of your employment.

Describe your level of knowledge and cultural sensitivity toward an underserved cultural group you are likely to work with. Develop a specific plan for developing cultural awareness and sensitivity toward at least one underserved minority cultural group.

_____

_____

_____

_____

_____

_____

_____

_____

_____

_____

_____

_____

_____

_____

_____

_____

_____

_____

CHAPTER 6

KNOW YOUR SKILL SET

Your *skill set* is the compilation of skills, knowledge, experience, and training that you have gained from various sources. The goal of this chapter is to help you develop an intimate knowledge of your objective worth as a future professional going into the field that is your goal. The skills, training, experience, and knowledge you have, which you may not be keenly aware of, include that gained from family members, past jobs, volunteering, life experiences, and from your classes. It is a shame that the average student or college graduate does not really know their worth. Without knowing your worth, you are less likely to compete for jobs or for entry into a graduate program. This chapter will help prompt you to think about various important places from which you are likely to have gained valuable job skills.

Family Members and Mentors

Family members, like parents, extended family, and informal mentors, are the first sources of knowledge introduced in our lives that help us prepare to become potentially successful professionals. Family members, especially parents, typically make efforts to teach their children skills such as deferred gratification, etiquette, and presenting yourself properly to others. Parents, for example, commonly dress their children well to attend church services or meaningful family gatherings. This conveys to a child that how we are presented to others reflects on the child and on the family. Similarly, employers put a lot of importance on the image conveyed by their employees that have implications for the image of the organization or company presented to others, like customers. Reflecting on the early experiences you have had and the principles conveyed by your parents can help you as an applicant to acknowledge those principles taught to you that can be used in a job interview for your benefit. For example, when asked in a job interview for, say, a job that works closely with customers, an applicant can say that they should be given the position in question because they hold important principles that they were taught by their parents, such as conveying courtesy and patience with others, that will make them better able to work with clients and customers. Perhaps you were taught to listen carefully to others, to empathize and understand. Conveying such early teachings that you uphold can perhaps land you the job you seek over others who simply talk about their formal education and job experiences.

Of course, not everyone's family members or parents are ideal role models. In fact, sometimes the opposite is true. You may have come from an abusive family or one where fights and conflict were the norm. These negative experiences can also provide you with special understanding, knowledge, and skills that others do not have that may prove to be important for jobs or graduate programs. For example, if you came from an abusive family and you have your degree, you can tell a panel of interviewers that you should get the job or entry into a graduate program because you are an overcomer or a resilient person. You know how to deal with conflict and work well under pressure. What is important is for you to make sure you understand the criteria used to choose an applicant for a job or graduate program and to identify those personal traits that you have that you can convey on an application or in an interview. This takes time, this introspective analysis of you and your background. Most of us are not immediately aware of the importance of our past experiences and how they are relevant to what we want professionally. Talking to those who know you and your background, such as siblings and confidants, can sometimes help you raise your awareness in this regard.

Life Experiences

Just like family experiences can help you, so can important past life experiences that are meaningful to you. Many students who gain their undergraduate degree are first-generation college students and commonly have faced social, economic, psychological, or family challenges and crises. These, sometimes traumatic, experiences shape and make us who we are. These challenging experiences are difficult to go through, but later in life they can have positive outcomes. For example, I came from a family where my parents fought constantly, seemingly yelling at each other all the time. Miraculously, they did not behave that way with their seven children, but boy were they mean with each other. Oddly enough, I learned to appreciate the good things that can come from such a dysfunctional family. I learned to appreciate and benefit from the love they conveyed to us children. This helped us to develop positive self-concepts, which, in turn, helped us to overcome challenges in life, including those at school. When you grow up in a dysfunctional family, you really do not know as you are growing up that your family is or was dysfunctional. You just seem to know that whatever happens is somehow "normal" even if in reality things are dysfunctional. My early experiences shaped me and made me who I am. Growing up in my particular dysfunctional family influenced my decision to become a psychologist, to study youth and families, and to do research on the development of prevention programs. Early on, I was not that conscious of how my early experiences influenced my educational or professional decisions. It was only later that I became aware of it, when I became a psychologist!

You too have been influenced and shaped by your early childhood experiences. Some—hopefully, most—experiences may be positive, but maybe some have been negative or challenging. Do an introspective study or reflection of yourself and of your early experiences to learn how your past has shaped you and, most importantly, what skills, knowledge, experience, and training you gained from those experiences that make you a better employee or graduate student in social, human or health fields. Maybe you can add an addendum to a *master resume*, a resume that is not directed to any particular job but is comprehensive (discussed further below), which you can use in applications or when interviewing. What is important is that you consider how your past experiences can help you better understand yourself and better understand how even challenging experiences have positive uses or outcomes in your future professional life. By the way, just because some of our families may have exhibited dysfunctional behaviors in some areas, we perhaps should not label them dysfunctional. Doing so ignores positive influences.

Past Jobs and Volunteer Experiences

Many times students will tell me they are having trouble preparing a resume for a job because they feel they do not have any meaningful professional experiences. They may have been waiters or waitresses, bartenders or baristas, or have worked in retail or at a grocery store. Having such "nonprofessional" jobs, they think that these jobs did not give them "professional" experiences that are worth noting on a resume. I quickly tell them how wrong they are in thinking this way since when working as a waitress or waiter, for example, you have to develop and practice customer service, problem solving, ability to work in teams, deal with accounting, and practice good interpersonal relationship and communication skills, to say the least. Think carefully about each job or volunteer experience you have and decipher what you could have gained from each in the areas of skills, knowledge, experience, or training that an employer or graduate program would be looking for in an applicant. Once you have properly mined your past experiences for these gains, list them in a master resume, which is not directed to any particular job but contains all that you can possibly list in an application. This master resume can then be used to prompt you as to what to include in an application or to discuss in a job interview.

Do the same with volunteer experiences. Include what you gained from such experiences in the master resume that you will refer to when forming a shorter and more targeted resume. When you consider your volunteer or job experiences, make sure that you note the populations you worked or interacted with, including ethnic or racial minorities, gender groups, age groups, economic groups, and so on. Also, make note of the skills you developed or demonstrated, including interpersonal relationship and communication skills. The point is to break down all that you gained from past job or volunteer experiences and include them in a master resume, which becomes a bank of knowledge of your worth as a future employee or graduate student.

The Worth of Your Classes

I will probably ask future students in my internship classes to go through their college transcript and to provide at least one to three marketable job skills, training, experiences, or knowledge gained from each class listed on their transcripts that any employer would want to know they gained from the classes taken. As students, we often look at the list of courses taken as simple requirements we can check off as we progress through our education without thinking about what the classes represent in terms of job skills, training, and knowledge gained. As we face a possible major recession with high unemployment, it becomes critical that you know *all* your worth based on everything you have done, including knowing well that which you gained from the classes you took.

After listing one to three job skills, knowledge, training, or experience gained from each of the classes taken, stand back and look at the list of things gained carefully. Given the job or graduate program you are applying for, point out those courses from the list that are worth mentioning in your application or interview that also perhaps complement your job experiences. I encourage you to also categorize classes that have taught or reinforced certain skills or knowledge. For example, many students in the social sciences will have taken a statistics and research methods course and possibly a course where they did some research, even it was focused on literature searches of particular topics. These courses had you do activities that can all come under the term *independent research skills* or *information gathering skills*, which many employers are impressed with and would love to see their potentially future employees have in order to solve problems or come up with innovations.

The important point of this chapter is to help you know your worth in terms of who you are and what you have gained from life experiences, your jobs or volunteer work, and the courses you took to get to where you are now. Make sure and develop your master resume so that you can understand those traits that make you special and allow you to stand out in any application. Remember, knowing your worth takes introspective reflection and a notation of those things you learned that make you special.

MY OWN NOTES AND REFLECTIONS ON CHAPTER 6

Questions and activities to consider, besides your own notes.

What significant life experiences have you had, be it traumatic or positive, that have helped you to be sensitive, aware, or enabled you to working with others?

Consider all the classes you have taken in college and develop a list of skills, experience, knowledge, and training that your classes provided you with that have prepared you for your career goal or goals.

Is there a particular expertise that you gained through your classes that you feel will impress an employer (e.g., from your ethnic or gender studies or social problem courses, etc.)?

Develop a list of skills, knowledge, training, and experience you gained from all the jobs you have had during and before college that any professional should have.

Plan on writing out your master resume that is comprehensive in listing out all the knowledge, training, skills, and experience you have gained through work, classes, life experiences, and from your own learning.

_____

_____

_____

_____

_____

_____

_____

_____

_____

_____

_____

_____

_____

_____

_____

_____

CHAPTER 7

KNOWING YOURSELF AS A RESILIENT OVERCOMER

As mentioned in previous chapters, there is value in past challenges you and your family have faced. Knowing and listing out those experiences allows you to be sensitive and understanding towards others, which is a valuable learning experience that most employers and graduate programs will appreciate. Many first-generation college graduating seniors have experienced challenges they have overcome or are using for their benefit, for example, to develop empathy. It is true that some challenges may have made you stronger, while others may have weakened you or limited you in some way. For instance, some students coming from substance-abusing families find that they cannot handle working in any way with those struggling with addictions because it brings back traumatic memories. They abhor being in the presence of addicted individuals, while others with the same background find that they want to work with families or individuals with addiction problems. They have a passion for working with such individuals. It is as if they are wanting to help as others had or had not in their own family. Both reactions are valid. You just need to be aware of your motives for working with whatever populations you seem to be interested in working with. Sometimes it is not the nature of the past experiences but rather the expectations that others have toward us that seem to influence our interests or plans for the future. My wife's mom was a nurse and her dad was a medical doctor. Their professions caused my wife to initially want to go into medicine or health care.

You also may find that you are interested in working with particular age groups, and upon reflection it may be because you needed a caring person like yourself to help you when you were growing up. When we are not aware of the past influences that drive our interests, we act unconsciously and do what psychologists call *unconscious projection*. We project ourselves onto others or their needs because we had those needs ourselves when we were that age or in that situation. Being aware of these influences is important because otherwise we feel emotionally overwhelmed trying to help or address, or worst, "solve" the problems of others, which, of course, we cannot.

Past problems and our need to help others who share our past problems cause us to develop what we call *savior syndrome*, where we want to help someone at any cost—often costing us undue stress and anxiety. For anyone who feels like you have a tendency to want to "fix" the problems of others at any cost, I recommend that you go see a therapist who can help you understand yourself and learn how your past experiences have shaped you and perhaps put you at risk of projecting your past problems onto others or of wanting to save people from their problems. A therapist can also help you understand how those same experiences have helped you to gain marketable job skills, knowledge, experience, and training that is influencing your career choice and is of value to you as you prepare for it. If you cannot or do not want to see a therapist, then find a trusted confidant and spend some time doing a retrospective evaluation of your past and how it is influencing your career interests. The main suggestion is for you to really know yourself, based on your upbringing and past experiences.

I mentioned earlier that I came from a family where parents fought night and day with each other. It was indeed very traumatic for me as a little kid seeing such verbal fighting, not knowing to what level the fights would escalate to, perhaps becoming physical, which, thankfully, they did not. That trauma led me to later, as a young adult, marry a person who was much like my father, someone who was critical of me just like my father was of my mother. We sometimes marry people like our parents and we do so to psychologically solve past problems, not knowing that it does not work that way. We can never fix someone—we have to accept them and learn to love with them as they are—or decide to not be with them. On the other hand, I have to accept the possibility that perhaps the person I married really was not like my father but rather that I treated her as if she was so (projection) and perhaps that really led to the role I assigned her, which led to our own conflict. The point is that we need to be aware of ourselves, of our past influences, and how it can be helpful if we go into in helping professions due to the empathy and special insight we may have of and toward others. But, as I explained, past challenges and experiences can also be destructive influences in our personal and professional life.

Acknowledge What You Have Overcome and Tie It to Your Resiliency

Overcoming past challenges can suggest that we are resilient people or survivors of past trauma or challenges. Being aware of our challenging experiences and traumas can help us convey understanding, sensitivity, and empathy when going through an interview or when writing a statement of purpose as part of a graduate school application. We are all survivors of past challenges in some way. Become aware of the challenges and trauma, list them out on paper, acknowledge them personally, and prepare to possibly mention them in applications or during interviews. Common experiences or challenges include low-income status, gender or cultural or racial bias or discrimination, bullying, and the like. Just be careful not to describe yourself in such a way that leads to pity or further bias. The way and context wherein you present your resilience given past trauma or challenges is as critical as the importance or value of such experience in the professional realm. Get guidance from trusted individuals who are not judgmental and biased themselves. They will guide you on the best way to present your resiliency and past trauma or challenges in life.

Benefits Coming from Your Gender or Cultural Background

It is unfortunate, but society continues to discriminate on the basis of gender and cultural or racial background, including skin color. As a result, even resilient students who are overcomers end up having low self-concepts or self-esteem and sometimes have what is called *imposter syndrome*, where you feel you do not deserve to be where you are or where you diminish yourself. Be aware of that, but also know the value of being a member of a particular gender, ethnic, or racial group. For example, being Hispanic or Mexican can make you not only able to sympathize with Hispanic and Mexican populations but also can allow you that special ability to empathize with others regardless of cultural background and really understand where people are coming from. Male students going into the nursing field that is dominated by females can use their gender to work with and empathize with male patients while also acknowledging that their perspective is unique and that they can benefit from being open to learning female perspectives. The point being that you should know the benefits that come from those cultural or gender characteristics that society often criticizes or minimizes and turn them into strengths instead of weaknesses.

This chapter complements the previous one but more specifically focuses on how your past experiences that may have been negative or even traumatic can lead to the development of skills and knowledge employers and graduate programs find of value. This understanding is particularly important for those going into human or health services. However, every field or occupation requires professionals to work with and understand one another. The trend now in companies is for employers to form small working groups that work together to solve problems or come up with innovative ideas. That includes companies that are in STEM fields (i.e., science, technology, engineering, and math). Regardless of the field, all employers need those who work well with and can understand others. I have emphasized negative or traumatic experiences, but it is equally important to recognize that positive experiences coming from loving and functional families are equally valuable and worthy of mentioning to potential employers as well. For example, if you were raised by a loving and cohesive family, you may mention to an employer how you learned from your family the importance of communication and working towards harmony even when challenges arise.

MY OWN NOTES AND REFLECTIONS
ON CHAPTER 7

Questions and activities to consider, besides your own notes.

What are some challenging experiences you have lived through that have made you a resilient overcomer? Focus on one challenging experience you lived through and explain how going through that experience has led to you having special knowledge, sensitivity, and awareness that you can use in working with populations in a human or health services job.

You do not have to be a cultural minority to realize that you have a culture. It may be a mixture of your parents' culture of origin that influenced you and/or tied you to an American culture rooted in your part of the country (e.g., Southern California or southern culture). Name your culture and list out the dominant beliefs, values, attitudes, and practices in that culture. Then write out how your cultural background helps you to work better in your chosen profession.

_____

_____

_____

_____

_____

_____

_____

_____

_____

_____

_____

_____

_____

_____

_____

_____

_____

_____

CHAPTER 8

KNOWING YOUR WEAKNESSES

U p to now, I have focused on knowing the strength that comes from past challenges that makes us resilient and gives us marketable job skills at the professional level. In this chapter, we deal with a more honest evaluation of ourselves that points to the weaknesses we have that we should acknowledge, try to change, or do away with altogether. We all have weaknesses. Some are personal, such as shyness, and others were caused by our environment or upbringing. Regardless, we all have them, and it is important for us to become aware of them. Let us consider common areas of weaknesses that can get in the way of developing our professional self.

Personal Weaknesses and Ways of Improving Them

Probably some of the most prevalent personal challenges that we experience has to do with low self-esteem or low self-concept. We may be in school, almost graduating or have already graduated, but we still might not hold ourselves in great esteem or feel that we have what it takes to apply for a job or to enter a competitive graduate program. I have told my students several times that the most critical person of us is ourselves. We often have had people in our past who have conveyed to us low expectations toward or appreciation of us that has led us to think less of ourselves. Sometimes the criticism is in particular areas we, too, acknowledge that we are weak in, but hearing it from others seems to validate those criticisms. For example, when I was a professor at Stanford University, we were asked as professors to meet with a minimum number of freshmen to welcome them. Incoming students would complete a questionnaire that would ask them about their experiences going through their education, which would influence their choice of major or classes they would look forward to taking at Stanford. Commonly, students would say something like they would not look forward to taking a math or biology class and definitely would not consider these as a potential majors because they had negative experiences, not just with the subject matter but with specific teachers who taught past classes and were critical of them.

Past challenging experiences with particular courses commonly lead students to do poorly in those classes or to have to work extra hard when taking them. Past criticisms from others affect the way we see ourselves. According to Bonnie Minsky, a certified life coach, you can do several things to overcome low self-concept, self-esteem, or negativity.[1] First, surround yourself with the right people who are positive, have healthy perspectives, and can validate you and acknowledge your worth and abilities. Having those who provide you with unconditional support is critical. Second, Minsky says you should try to "get to know yourself/become your own best friend." That is where creating a master resume can aide in helping you know your worth (see previous chapter). Also, list out your personal characteristics that make you special, such as being caring, empathetic, diligent, hardworking, sensitive, understanding, a good listener, or a loyal friend, among many other traits. Talk with confidants and ask them to help you complete a list of personal characteristics that make you special. Look at them to learn to appreciate your personal characteristics.

Third, acknowledge areas where you need to change. It is a sad and simple truth that if you came from a poor neighborhood or background, you likely came from a school that did not prepare you well for college. You likely have a challenge with writing and probably with speaking too. Employers and graduate programs require that university-level graduates have good writing skills. That means that graduates should be able to write without grammatical or spelling errors and be able to convey their thoughts clearly in writing. This is important because, in today's world, we seem to rely more and more on abbreviated writing through electronic communication means, such as through emails and text messages. Unfortunately, text and email writing sometimes weakens our ability to write complete sentences. Writing is a skill that no one is born with. Being a skill, it is improved through training and practice. Reading helps us to recognize good writing and allows us to be exposed to a greater vocabulary. If you find it difficult to write, then practice doing so and take a writing class, if possible. If anything, make sure that when you put together an application, you have others read it before submitting it. I do not think I have ever written even a short email where I did not see errors that needed to be corrected. I notice that when I write, my mind thinks of the sentence I wish to write, but my hand finds it difficult to keep up with the mind, and as a result, I end up omitting words that I needed to complete the sentence.

Oral Communication

The other skill that is important in the professional world that we need to be sure we know where we stand is our ability to speak clearly. Oral speaking sounds simple, but let me assure you that it is not—my wife knows this very well. Oral communication involves taking the time to clearly communicate what you mean to say. Communicating effectively entails asking questions of your audience to make sure they capture your intended thoughts and messages.[2] Communication is a two-way street where one speaks while the other listens and then the listener speaks while the speaker listens. Before you speak, make sure your listener's mind is not expecting something different or is in some other mental state. When I was a researcher for the navy, I applied for a grant to the central naval command to undertake a worldwide study of navy personnel to see whether what happens in a military member's personal life and family affects their job performance, readiness, and retention. I was so nervous and worried that perhaps I did not turn in a strong, competitive application. On one particular day, I was told that our commanding officer at the center was possibly getting the news of the acceptance or rejection of my application. I was eager to know and get some news on the outcome of my application.

There was a snack shop on the naval base where we all would go to get coffee and snacks. While nervous about my grant application, I decided to go get a cup of coffee before going to ask the commanding officer about my application. There I saw a fellow peer named John who was also a researcher who was also getting something from the snack bar. He was African American and just a very nice person to run into. The conversation went like this:

I asked, "Hey, how's it going with you John?!"

John replied, "I'm mighty fine, and you?"

I returned with, "Oh, I'm fine."

John exclaimed, "I heard that!"

"John, really? Where'd you hear that?" (Because of my worry over my proposal, I assumed that he was telling me something he heard about my grant.)

He looked at me funny, and I mistook his puzzled look to mean he was nonverbally saying, "Well, you mean you don't know about the outcome of your grant proposal review?"

So, I physically followed (really stalked him) John, asking, "No really, really John, where'd you hear that??"

It was not until later that I remembered that "I heard that" is a common refrain especially used by some African Americans with no particular meaning tied to the refrain, except to just be friendly. So the point is, make sure that you and those you are conversing with have the same frame of mind. You do that by using reflective listening. For instance, I could have said, "John, are you saying 'I heard that' because you heard about the outcome of my research application? I can't get that application out of my mind!"

To improve your oral speaking ability, I highly recommend that you join a Toast-masters group. Toastmasters is an organization that promotes small meetings of professionals who learn to give talks, to communicate, and to do formal presentations. They teach each other communication principles and give you a chance to practice speaking while you can also listen to others present, as well. There are many such groups throughout the United States, and all you need to do is to find the one nearest to you. Many attend these meetings during their lunchbreak. To find one, go the Toastmaster's website (https://www.toastmasters.org/). These meetings are also excellent ways of networking with professionals who can help you find professional jobs.

This chapter is important in that it acknowledges that we all have weaknesses that can affect our success as professionals. Knowing them is a critical first step in addressing them. Writing and speaking are two important skills that you need to have and improve on. The times I have spoken with employers where I ask them what they look for when hiring professionals, they invariably put writing and speaking as top skills they look for. Being skills, you need to learn and develop or enhance them. There are other weaknesses, such as having a low self-concept or self-esteem, that can also influence our success as professionals. For many, simply recognizing your worth by documenting your strengths and traits can help. For others, seeing a therapist is important for getting help with improving a self-concept or self-esteem. A therapist can help you acknowledge and accept your positive attributes and traits.

Notes

1. Minsky, B. (2018, October 22). *How to overcome low self-esteem and negativity: Low self-esteem and pessimism can make it difficult to accept responsibility and constructive criticism.* Thrive Global. https://thriveglobal.com/stories/how-to-overcome-low-self-esteem-and-negativity/
2. Geikhman, Y. (n.d.). 8 Essential tips for clear communication in English. *FluentU.* https://www.fluentu.com/blog/english/english-communication-tips/

MY OWN NOTES AND REFLECTIONS ON CHAPTER 8

We all have weaknesses. What do you consider to be the weaknesses you may be able to improve on to augment your professional success?

What is your level of writing ability and attention to detail? Assuming that you now have your degree and are considered a professional, how prepared are you to give oral presentations? Regardless of level of proficiency, develop a plan for improving your writing and speaking abilities.

CHAPTER 9

DEVELOPING YOUR PROFESSIONAL PERSONA

M y students have heard me talk about them needing to develop their new professional persona after graduation. We all have various *personas*, or identities. We are sons or daughters, sisters or brothers, Catholic, Methodist, Californian, San Diegan, of German or Irish background, African American, Mexican American, Korean, Chinese, Navajo, or college students, and right now maybe a graduating senior. All these categories and roles have specific identities, or personas, that have their own way of talking, relating to others, or of being. For example, when it is Thanksgiving and you go home to your parents' house, if you think about it, you likely start acting a bit childish, like a younger son or daughter, with your parents. We tend to revert to the earlier role of us being kids. You may typically have mom or dad do the cooking while you rest and be waited on. The way you talk, intonate, dress, and even your posture usually complement that younger role. Of course, not all experience this, but many do. The same holds true when you are at university. There you are a student, specifically, maybe a graduating senior. As such, you will talk the way college students talk, with slang words like dude or bro usually being a big part of what you say. Your attire commonly is casual, possibly with a school sweatshirt or t-shirt with the school's logo on it.

In the same way, after graduation you need to find your own professional persona. You can either haphazardly develop it or sometimes someone else assigns it to you: "Oh yeah, you need to always have to push Bobby to get things done." If you are not careful, you will be pushed to the back room, so to speak, where no one cares about you or you can take control and develop the person or persona you *wish* to be. List out the main traits you want to be known for as a professional and assign dress, posture, voice, and intonation to it. At your university, if you are still a student, you will have access to the career center, many of which give students access to an interactive web-based interview program called Big Interview.[1] Through it you can record yourself and go through mock interviews that are videotaped. Regardless of whether you have access to Big Interview or not, make it a point to watch videos of yourself acting out your professional persona and use the videos to develop the professional persona you wish to attain. Then try using it with your trusted confidants, going through mock verbal interviews or job-setting interactions. Make sure to have professional dress associated with the new persona. Make your attire clearly professional. For guys, a coat, dress shirt, pants, and tie. For women, wear a formal, professional dress (not club dress!) or skirt with a formal white or off-white long sleeve blouse. Have the clothing or attire speak to you visually, telling you and others that you are not the college student anymore. You are now a professional—be it a scientist, researcher, engineer, social worker, nurse, case manager, youth worker, youth counselor, or whatever you aspire to be.

Attend professional meetings and presentations at universities, colleges, or businesses where you can network while you are practicing your new professional persona. Universities often have such events listed on their websites. When you do attend these events, even if they are on college campuses where students wear informal attire, dress professionally. Pay attention to your voice and posture. When you talk, generate a professional, but friendly, voice with inflections and avoid using a monotone voice. Practice your voice. Men, practice imitating a student voice and contrast it with what you would consider a professional voice so that you know the contrast. Similarly, women need to pay keen attention to their own voice. Your voice should reflect a commanding presence that sounds like you are sure of yourself. Do the same and practice your voice as a female student, contrasting it with your new professional voice. Keep your body straight and convey a semblance of calm and control. After you have decided on your professional voice and posture, practice it with trusted friends or family members. Also, listen to others who you feel reflect a professional persona, learning as much as you can from them. Prepare an elevator pitch ahead of any professional event you attend, which includes determining answers to common questions people have of you:

- **Who you are and where you are from:** "Hi, my name is Mary and I am originally from Atlanta, Georgia, but am now living in San Francisco."
- **What you are doing there or where you are going:** "I am here to attend a job fair to see what opportunities there are in my field."
- **Your Field and Career Interests:** "I have a degree in Human Development, which is an interdisciplinary social science field, and I am interested in finding a job in case management working with families."

Relating Interpersonally

As you develop your professional persona, make sure you learn the skill of relating interpersonally with other professionals. This does not come automatically but rather it is a skill that is developed with experience, and sometimes through professional training. Being that it is a skill, you will make mistakes and errors as you learn to improve your ability to relate to other professionals interpersonally. Making mistakes is normal and is fine, but make sure to learn from them to avoid them in the future. Relating well interpersonally means that you will practice and learn the following skills.

Learn to Listen

If you are shy by nature, you probably will find it easier to practice this skill. But when I say "listening" I do not mean staying quiet. There are many shy people who fail to listen and are only good at being silent. Listening means that you understand what a speaker is saying. Contrary to introverts, extroverts often find it easy to always talk. For extroverts, the listening skill is likely to be a challenge for you, and you will need to spend time learning this skill that may go against your natural interpersonal tendency to always speak. Interestingly, listening can be a more important skill than speaking. Abraham Lincoln said that it was, "Better to remain silent and be thought a fool than to speak and to remove all doubt." So, learn the art of listening, which includes reflective listening, where you repeat what you think you heard. For example: "So I hear you saying that Dr. Soriano is great when you say he is the bomb?"

Take Personal Interest in Professionals You Meet

When you attend professional meetings or come across professionals, take interest in those you are meeting. Ask them questions and learn from them. Showing interest in professionals leads to people taking an interest in you and in helping you reach your professional goals. It leads to good networking and to an enhanced list of people you can count on in the future for advice or to helping you meet others in their professional circle. An especially helpful piece of advice is to learn the art of showing an interest in others without conveying false personal or romantic interest. Remember to keep boundaries. Keeping the focus in conversations on professional topics helps in this regard. Also, mentioning your spouse or significant other will help you to be clear that you are communicating as professionals. Showing proper interest in professionals you meet does take practice.

Practice Ping-Pong Conversations

Practice what I call *ping-pong conversations*. Start with you requesting information: "Hi, my name is ___. What is yours?" After your initial question, wait attentively for their response. Afterwards, provide them with some information about you, such as "I recently graduated and I am looking for a job as case manager," followed by yet another inquiry about the professional: "You say you are an engineer. How do you like working as a structural engineer?" which is followed by you giving them additional information about yourself, and so forth. The idea is to never let one person provide most of the information and dominate the conversation. That way you will be acknowledged, and a relationship will start in earnest and with interpersonal knowledge.

Convey Humility in a Context of Strength and Worth

When meeting with professionals, demonstrate modesty and professional humility but not humiliation or lowliness. By humility I mean do not brag and do not look down on or criticize others. Have solid reasons why you have professional worth, based on your field, but do not diminish others. That is why doing the assessment of your worth, as mentioned in Chapter 6, is so important. Have your elevator pitch ready with the list of traits that make you personally and professionally special. That allows you to show humility and approachability, which conveys solid professional strength and worth.

Developing your professional persona takes effort and focus. No one graduating with their degree should assume they are ready to step on a conveyer belt to success without working on establishing the person you are professionally—your professional persona. I often tell my students, whether they want to or not, they will each become actors in the professional world, actors who define a particular professional person who has particular traits that include self-assurance and openness to developing healthy relationships with other professionals. You will need to practice the specific skills mentioned in this chapter that will make you successful. So plan on putting in the time to develop your skills and traits that will form that unique professional persona that is *you* in the professional realm.

Note

1. *Big Interview* available through CSUSM's Career Center website: https://www. csusm.edu/careers/careerservices/practice_interviews.html

MY OWN NOTES AND REFLECTIONS
ON CHAPTER 9

To what extent have you developed your professional persona? What kind of professional do you want to be known as? Write out a description of your professional persona, noting those distinctive qualities you wish others to notice, which can include dress, voice, ability to listen, and posture. Identify any other area you wish to improve on as you develop your professional persona.

What is your elevator pitch? It could be helpful to write it out, but you should also rehearse saying it out loud, perhaps in front of a mirror or to a confidant.

_____

_____

_____

_____

_____

_____

_____

_____

_____

_____

_____

_____

_____

_____

_____

_____

_____

_____

_____

_____

_____

_____

CHAPTER 10

IMPORTANCE OF SOCIAL SUPPORT AND SOCIAL NETWORKS

Humans are social by nature and we depend on the interaction and support of others. The closer we are to people, the more we depend on them for such things as:

- **Conversation:** As social creatures, it is vital that we have people to talk to for the joy that comes from talking and listening.
- **Opinions and Advice:** It is always helpful to have the opportunity to talk to others to discuss problems/challenges/opportunities and solutions. Similarly, we seek wise counsel to get advice to come up with solutions to problems or make decisions.
- **Empathy:** We often seek out the presence of others to get support when we are sad, anxious, stressed, or depressed. Also, when we face rejections or challenges in life.
- **Happiness, Joy, and Celebration:** We also look to share our happiness with others. Doing so seems to make our happiness and joy that much greater. This includes celebrating accomplishments and successes with others, which makes our success that much more special.
- **Entertainment and Activities:** Doing activities with others is so much more fun than doing things alone. We love hanging out with others, like friends, that we can do things with, including attending ceremonies or community events.
- **Tangible Assistance:** Finally, we sometimes call on others to help us with material assistance, including financial support, housing, and childcare.

There are many who surround us who can provide some or many of the benefits listed above. That includes our immediate family, extended family, friends of the family, close peers we grew up with or went to school with, friends, neighbors, community members and agency workers, teachers/professors, and mentors. In low-income populations, it is not uncommon to have neighbors or friends of the family take over as surrogate parents when the parent(s) are not able to care for their children due to work schedules. My wife, for example, was raised largely by an aunt because her mother was always busy working as a nurse. Sometimes in large cities with high population density, like New York or Chicago, people end up developing a casual, but very important, relationship with service workers, such as outdoor produce merchants or hot dog cart attendants. The point is that, as human beings, we have lots of people that we depend on, and these different types of people or groups comprise what we can consider our social support or network.

Social Support Versus Social Networks

Allow me to make a distinction between social support systems and social networks. Social support systems include those that we currently derive some benefit from. Our social support can be general or specific. Overall, social support systems are those that usually encompass our intimate circle, which includes family, friends, and others that play an active role in our lives on a daily basis in all aspects and dimensions in our life. It includes those coworkers, close friends, and companions. A social support system draws from our *social network*, which consists of all available sources of people that can be engaged in any aspect of our life at any point in time. The bigger the social network, the more you are able to develop social support groupings that meet specific needs, such as those we can count on for childcare and parenting. Another social support group can be drawn from our broader employment-related social network, which can include coworkers and peers who encourage us and who support our success in the workplace.

If we go through a serious economic downturn or trend, we need to take stock of our social networks that we can draw support and assistance from. Take time to acknowledge your social support networks in various realms, including family, extended family, friends, acquaintances, school peers, coworkers, neighbors, college support program staff or counselors, past teachers, and professors. Plan on building a social support network that you can draw specialized help from. This requires you (1) to be ready to continually add individuals to your social network, (2) make an ongoing effort to recruit network members, and (3) maintain regular contact with those in your existing network by keeping them actively aware, engaged, and interested in you and your well-being. Career, job, or college networks will be particularly important for you to develop. If you find yourself unemployed, try not to stay home but rather take advantage of any training opportunities that the government or community organizations offer. Attend relevant presentations and meetings (virtually or in person), and at these meetings, strike up conversations with people to develop relationships with them. As mentioned before, when indicating interest in others, be sure that the message is clear that you are not interested in a romantic relationship but rather a professional relationship that can lead to developing camaraderie.

Importance of Family of Origin

A family of origin is the family you grew up with. For those who grew up in the foster care system, it is usually the family or families you spent the most time living with or the last family that you lived with before aging out of the system. Family of origin members play a particularly important role since, unlike friends or peers, they know you well due to a shared history, having been present for your early childhood experiences. What they say, whether positive or negative, has added weight, which makes their judgements and opinions that much more important and impactful. You may have had a terrible relationship with a parent or foster parent, but oddly enough, what they say to you, even after you have discounted them, still impacts you. So be careful to limit your contact with those who can be a negative influence or detract you from your goal of succeeding professionally.

Sometimes even challenging family members are able to provide support to you in some ways, such as with financial support. Learn to take any positive support that family offers and limit how you react to any negative influences that sometimes comes from even generally loving family members. Try to resist resentment when family members refuse to help in specific areas, mindful that they may be able to help in other areas. The average family, overall, bears a very positive influence and impact on our lives. During financial challenges, families become particularly important since they are more likely to share resources and provide support, such as childcare.

In times of economic downturns or recessions, broad members of society are affected and deprived of resources they used to have. Families are no different. Be sensitive to your parents' or guardians' own limitations of resources, careful not to expect too much from them since they are also likely being adversely impacted by the economic downturn. What you do not want is for the economic stress that comes with recessions to create tensions, dissensions, or divisions within the family that will cause you to stop benefitting from the emotional and practical support you would otherwise receive. Having said that, do seek out support from your family of origin—emotional and/or material—when it is available. I remember when I was an undergraduate, when I was stressed over an exam that I felt I did not do as well in, I would go home, and because they never went to college, my parents always welcomed me unconditionally and would say something like, "Don't worry about it. Just offer it up to God. He will help you. Here, have something to eat." Beyond the words, I *felt* their support and validation of me regardless of my performance in school or even in my social life. Many families or relatives offer such support. Seek it out, if available. It will help you cope with stressors you are confronting.

Immediate Family or Intimate Relationships

What is true about families of origin, is also true about our immediate families or intimate relationships—that is, those who we are living with, married to, or otherwise. Couples without children may be considered families or not. That is subjective. If you have children, then you have certainly started an immediate family. Immediate families are even more important than families of origin because you typically spend more time with them than you do with families of origin. Therefore, you need to be sure to protect your immediate family from the natural tensions and stressors that typically come with recessions due to resource scarcity and challenging experiences tied to unemployment or underemployment.

I had one student majoring in human development who was a graduating senior with the goal of becoming a social worker or case manager working with families. He lost his job due to the COVID-19 pandemic crisis. His wife was the only one earning any income. He found himself as a homemaker unable to find employment. He provided childcare for their five-year-old and had the responsibility of doing all the housekeeping even as he continued with finishing up his last semester before graduating at the university. He acknowledged the undue stress that the pandemic crisis was causing him and his wife. He had a hard time caring for his 5-year-old, because the child sought constant attention from him. One suggestion I offered to him was to not view his time caring for his daughter as "wasted" or as a challenging time but rather to see it as an opportunity to learn about child development from his observations of her, which can translate into a knowledge-based skill regarding the behavioral and cognitive manifestations of preschool childhood development. Whether in an application or interview he can talk about how he witnessed normative and non-normative development of preschool children in preparation for becoming a social worker.

You will do well to do the same and to translate all challenges and experiences into positive learning and training experiences, which you can add to the list of all your other job or career-related skills, qualifications, and knowledge. By changing your perspective on challenging tasks or situations, you can enhance your mood and outlook, making you feel more positive and hopeful. This, combined with practical action, can guard your immediate family from undue stress and anxiety that often leads to tension and discord. If it gets to that point, consider reaching out for help from family or a marriage therapist.

Importance of Friends

Friends play an important role in providing you with support, advice, and information that can help you make necessary decisions. Friendships can range from being "bosom friends" or "soulmates" to casual "I barely know your name" kind of friends. I remember that when I was an undergraduate at the University of California, Riverside, I loved going to the library to study, and I often ran into a peer that I never had a class with but who was always very friendly. She introduced herself the first day I met her. Lazy as I was to remember names, I did not capture her name. She, on the other hand, learned my name right away and would always greet me with, "Hi, Fernando!!!" Because she already introduced herself and gave me her name, I was too embarrassed to ask for her name. For all the years I was at UC Riverside getting my undergraduate degree, I never learned her name. It was not until about seven years ago—many years after graduating—that I visited UC Riverside to attend a meeting there that I ran into her! She was cheerful as ever, right away mentioning my name, which she did not forget. I had to confess to her that I had forgotten her name, and it was only then that I learned that her name was Joanne! Of course, I did not tell her that I actually had never learned her name but rather made it seem like it was only a momentary lapse in my memory. The point of sharing this story was not to confess to you a grievous fault (though it probably was a secondary reason) but rather to tell you that, while I did not learn her name, she played an important role as a friend. Every time we talked in front of the library over those four years at school, I always looked forward to talking to her to learn from her about her experiences going through school, taking classes that I had taken or was about to take. She really was a nameless good friend for all those years.

Clearly, there are friends that are closer to us than others, but all play an important role and form part of our social network from which we can draw support. As we go into a possible recession, friends at all levels will play critical roles in: (1) helping us to not feel alone, (2) obtaining helpful information and advice, (3) acting as a sounding board where we can share what we are going through instead of keeping it all inside, (4) giving us options on things to do or accompany us to events and activities that entertain us and distract us from the stress of our situation, and, most importantly, (5) providing us with leads on jobs and other opportunities.

In a separate manuscript I am currently writing, I make the case that outside of relatives, people in our sphere generally fit into seven different levels of support that, when combined, are all critical to our mental health and well-being and comprise our social support system. Members of our social support system range from casual, basic acquaintances, such as the attendant at your local 7-Eleven, to close, personal friends and, of course, intimates or confidants and companions. Below are the levels I have identified, which give you an idea of the various levels of social support that one can have, which makes up our social support system as a whole.

Level One: Simple or Basic Acquaintances—These are those people you casually meet in your realm or neighborhood (e.g., convenience store workers, hair dressers, etc.). Conversations here are limited to just greetings, but familiarity with each other does convey a sense of belonging and care.

Level Two: Casual Acquaintances—These are people you meet and have a casual conversation with. They likely know your name and have some knowledge of you, but the depth of knowledge is limited. Such people can be colleagues or coworkers, but the interactions with them stay distant and are not personal.

Level Three: Personal Acquaintances—These people know you relatively well. They know you by name and know who you are, generally. These could include neighbors and some coworkers who you get to know better. Their knowledge is nonetheless not deep nor extensive.

Level Four: Community Friends—These are people who you may interact with more frequently and do things with in the community. These can be close neighbors where you regularly help each other when need arises or can be clubs, like bike clubs or advocacy groups helping worthy causes. They are people you know relatively well, but the contact is limited to particular roles each have in the community.

Level Five: Practical Friends and Family—These can include tennis or golfing friends. You know each other by name, and they have relatively more knowledge of you, but there is no expectation of being confidants. These people clearly earn the title of friends because you hang out with them regularly. These can be relatives, coworkers, members of a group you a part of, or school peers.

Level Six: Personal Friends and Family—Unlike practical friends and family, personal friends know you well and are always there to call on when you need help or advice. They know you well and can ask you about how you are doing in various realms, including work, school, and intimate relationships. You can easily share with them personal or relationship challenges. They give you support and advice when you need it. They can be relatives or not.

Level Seven: Intimate Friends or Companions—The only difference between personal friends and intimate friends or companions is the level of intimacy and trust you have with them. These intimate friends or companions are those you share more intimate information and concerns with. They can be childhood friends or they can be your companions, such as spouse or partner. These are the ones whose words and advice make the most difference to you.

The purpose in listing these levels is to make you aware of the various people around you that comprise your social support system. Even at the more basic level, the grocery store cashier may be someone you feel grateful for because you always greet each other and seem to appreciate one another. The list can also be used to assess the extent to which you have people at the different levels. The more people you easily recognize as fitting into each level, the greater your social support system that you can call on when things get rough in your life. You can target recruiting people in particular levels that you may be lacking.

If things get difficult with unemployment or with finances, you can use this list to think of those who you can call upon for advice or practical assistance. Financial hardships can lead to elevated stress and anxiety, which often leads to the tendency for us to isolate ourselves, particularly from those who are dear to us for fear of worrying others or of being criticized. If that happens and you feel the urge to isolate yourself, use the basic, lower levels of friendship listed above to break out of the isolation. This will allow you to push yourself to interact with those at higher relationship levels because at the higher levels are those that will have a higher impact in you, on finding solutions to problems—these include your family members and close friends.

Supervisors, Counselors, and Professors as Mentors

According to the National Academies of Sciences, Engineering, and Medicine, a mentor is a "wise and trusted counselor."[1] A mentor is someone who has enough experience and knowledge to help you and that you can call on to give you wise advice. Many of you may have had the experience of having at least one mentor, be it a teacher, counselor, supervisor, or professor. The person being mentored is called a protégé. The protégé may have initiated the mentorship or the mentor may have seen something special in you that prompted them to want to help you educationally or professionally. If you do not have a current mentor, try to find one, perhaps reaching out to past professors, teachers, or counselors.

Studies on resiliency show that many who are considered to be resilient and have overcome past trauma, commonly had one or more mentors—people who believed in them and saw something special in them that others did not. Such studies suggest that mentors can have a significant impact on others and can change their life course for the better. You need to know that you can prompt significant people to become mentors and supporters of you by you developing relationships with them. For example, I have gotten to know students even more during the pandemic in Zoom class sessions. I usually get onto a Zoom session a few minutes before class starts. During those early minutes before class, I have been able to engage students in casual conversations and that has led to me getting to know the students better, which, in turn, has led to me starting mentorship relationships with some of them.

You need to know that you have control over the possibility of developing mentorship relationships. If you respect a professor, counselor, or teacher, engage them in conversation and ask them for advice on questions you have regarding your career, continued education, or whatever you need help with. Spend time with them and get to know them. When I say time, it does not necessarily mean doing it in person. Email them or have a phone or Zoom conversation with them. Mentors, like teachers, counselors, professors, or supervisors, know a lot of people who can potentially help you. You can develop mentorship relationships even after you graduate from school.

This chapter has emphasized the importance of people the around you who can serve as your social and practical support. Most successful people have reached success as a result of receiving help from others. Family plays the most important role in early life, but forming bonds with those not related to you is the key to continued success as an adult. Mentors are important people who can use their experience and wisdom to help guide you and overcome obstacles to your professional success. It is important for you to know that even if you do not recognize it, you *do* have a social support network from which to derive your social support system. This system is made up of people that vary in terms of their knowledge and level of interaction with you. Taken as a whole, the individuals in your system are those that help you get over challenges and help you find solutions to problems. Become familiar with those in your social network and recognize those that form your social support system who can help you achieve whatever professional goal you may have.

Note

1. Institute of Medicine, National Academy of Sciences, and National Academy of Engineering. (1997). *Adviser, teacher, role model, friend: On being a mentor to students in science and engineering.* National Academies Press. https://doi.org/10.17226/5789.

MY OWN NOTES AND REFLECTIONS ON CHAPTER 10

Questions and activities to consider, besides your own notes.

Who are your confidants, persons you can count on to listen to you about personal concerns and get advice from?

Describe your current social support network and social support system. Identify strengths you have with your network and weaknesses in terms of its breadth.

Develop a plan for constructing a more complete social support network and support groups that are there to help you personally and professionally. Identify at least three mentors you have who can serve as professional supporters of you and can give you good letters of recommendation or at least help serve as references. If you do not have strong professional supporters or mentors, develop a plan for developing them over the next few weeks.

_____

_____

_____

_____

_____

_____

_____

_____

_____

_____

_____

_____

_____

_____

_____

_____

_____

_____

_____

PART III

TAKING ACTION AND MAKING DECISIONS

CHAPTER 11

UNDERSTANDING THE ECONOMY AND ITS RELEVANCE TO THE JOB MARKET

National and Regional Differences

Toward the beginning of this book, I defined what an economic recession is so that you understand how it affects the challenges you will likely face during a severe recession or economic downturn. Now I will present information that is important in preparation for taking action. In preparing for action you need to study and be sure to understand national, regional, and local trends in the economy and employment. As mentioned earlier, the U.S. Department of Labor uses rapidly climbing unemployment rates as a key indicator of a recession. According to a report from the Department of Labor, during the Great Recession of 2007–2009, the unemployment rate doubled, going from 5% in December 2007 to 10% in October 2009.[1] According to the federal government, an unemployed person is one who has been actively looking for a job over the past four weeks and is currently available to be employed. The unemployment rate is the number of unemployed people as a percentage of the total labor force. The total labor force includes the unemployed.

There is another number, or proportion, of the labor force that is also important and may be vital to keep track of since that proportion shows how intractable or challenging the recession is. That proportion is of the *long-term unemployed*, those who have been unemployed the previous 27 weeks or more, as a percentage of the total labor force.[2] The higher the rates of unemployed and long-term unemployed, the more likely it is that you will face challenges finding employment. Also, the more challenging it is to land a professional job, the more likely it is that those with undergraduate degrees will seek graduate degrees as a way of waiting out a recession as they enhance their education and, consequently, their employability.

Knowing the Jobs/Careers Most Adversely Affected or That Are in Demand in Your Area

The national unemployment rates are important to note, but more important are the local or regional rates in your area. Using San Diego County as an example, during the Great Recession, unemployment was largely the same in San Diego County, for example, as it was for the nation (9.9.7% San Diego County, 10.1% national).[3] Now let's look at how unemployment rates in San Diego County were affected by the 2020 pandemic. In February 2020, San Diego County enjoyed an unemployment rate of 3.2%; by March it crept up to 4.1%.[4,5] According to SANDAG, the unemployment rate increased to 24.7% in April 2020.[6] A map of unemployment as of April 18, 2020, in San Diego County by zip code shows the discrepancy across the region. It is this detailed analysis in your own region that you need to pay attention to when applying for jobs in order to know where they are located geographically.[7] The same map for the San Diego region shows that employment in the whole region has been significantly and adversely affected. It also shows that the zip codes with more affluent incomes tend to fare better than those with lower incomes, such as those along the international border with Mexico like East County and Southwest County.[8] The San Diego County example shows how even in one county there are regional differences that need to be considered. This is the kind of analysis you need to do for your own region, which will help you know the challenges and/or opportunities you have in your own region and state.

It was one of my students who cited a Department of Labor report during a class discussion in which it was reported that the most promising areas of employment observed during the Great Recession of 2007–2009 were in the health and education sectors.[9] We are beginning to see that those same career sectors are increasingly promising during our current economy at present, particularly given the fact that the current economic status was sparked by a health crisis that is demanding a lot from our health care systems. In the same way, the current health crisis pandemic has also caused school districts throughout the country to teach remotely. The necessity of remote teaching is leading to an increased need for staff and personnel with expertise in the use of technology in education. This is the kind of helpful information that you should look for when searching for professional employment opportunities in growing sectors of the economy.

Use your analysis of what you have gained from your education and past employment, as mentioned in earlier chapters, to establish your employment worth and ability to match employment requirements in emerging fields of the economy. However, for those who do not want to get just *any* job and really want to focus on their own professional field or area of interest, you will need to consider some things. First, collect information regarding the job market and the hiring being done in the fields of interest in the geographic area where you wish to work. Continuing to use the San Diego region as an example, the San Diego Association of Governments, known as SANDAG,[10] has representation from the various cities in San Diego County, and part of its charge is to collect demographic and job-related data from various municipal, state, and federal government sectors and analyzes these for the benefit of cities and regions within the county. Many regions throughout the United States have similar regional intergovernmental organizations that you should look up. They are a good source of information, covering many subject areas, including employment trends. Another important source of information on specific careers and jobs is the *Occupational Outlook Handbook* that the Department of Labor makes available for free online,[11] which can give you information on specific careers, jobs, and related occupations, including their level of demand and required qualifications. It breaks down information by region, which is extremely helpful. Be aware that during major recessions, some of the information coming from such sources on jobs and occupations may not be current, especially when dramatic changes in the economy result from emerging major recessions.

This chapter emphasizes several things. One is for you to consider the changes in the job market in your specific region of the country. It is important to know which economic sectors are depressed in your area, such as those in the service/hospitality sector, and which are actually growing, such as in the health and education sectors. Given these changes in the economy, you have to decide whether you follow the economy or whether you continue with your career goal despite the challenges in finding jobs in those fields. If you choose the latter, you will succeed *if* you carefully align your past education, experience, and training with the requirements of the professional occupations of interest. There are data and policy organizations, such as SANDAG in the San Diego region, that can help you get accurate and timely information on emerging employment needs in your region. The federal government also has valuable information that can help you understand the emerging job markets and the desired qualifications for these in your state and region. Information will always help you make decisions and choices.

Notes

1. U.S. Bureau of Labor Statistics. (2012). *Spotlight on statistics: The recession of 2007–2009*. U.S. Department of Labor. The Recession of 2007–2009: BLS Spotlight on Statistics.

2. U.S. Bureau of Labor Statistics. (2012). *Spotlight on statistics: The recession of 2007–2009*. U.S. Department of Labor. URL: https://data.bls.gov/cgi-bin/print.pl/ spotlight/2012/recession/home.htm

3. U.S. Bureau of Labor Statistics. (2021, February 3). *Unemployment rate in San Diego County, CA* [CASAND5URN]. Retrieved from FRED, Federal Reserve Bank of St. Louis, at https://fred.stlouisfed.org/series/CASAND5URN

4. U.S. Bureau of Labor Statistics. (2021, February 3). *Unemployment rate in San Diego County, CA* [CASAND5URN]. Retrieved from FRED, Federal Reserve Bank of St. Louis, at https://fred.stlouisfed.org/series/CASAND5URN

5. State of California, Labor Market Information Division. (2020). *San Diego-Carlsbad metropolitan statistical area (San Diego County)*. https://www.labormarketinfo.edd.ca.gov/file/lfmonth/sand$pds.pdf

6. San Diego Association of Governments. (2020). *Update: COVID-19 impact on the San Diego regional economy: Employment analysis: Unemployment by zip code: Estimated unemployment by zip code as of April 18, 2020*. https://www.sandag.org/uploads/publicationid/publicationid_4660_27406.pdf

7. San Diego Association of Governments. (2020). *Update: COVID-19 impact on the San Diego regional economy: Employment analysis: Unemployment by zip code: Estimated unemployment by zip code as of April 18, 2020*. https://www.sandag.org/uploads/publicationid/publicationid_4660_27406.pdf

8. San Diego Association of Governments. (2020). *Update: COVID-19 impact on the San Diego regional economy: Employment analysis: Unemployment by zip code: Estimated unemployment by zip code as of April 18, 2020*. https://www.sandag.org/uploads/publicationid/publicationid_4660_27406.pdf

9. U.S. Bureau of Labor Statistics. (2012). *Spotlight on statistics: The recession of 2007–2009*. U.S. Department of Labor. https://data.bls.gov/cgi-bin/print.pl/spotlight/2012/recession/home.htm

10. San Diego Association of Governments. (n.d.). *About*. https://www.sandag.org/index.asp?fuseaction=about.home

11. Bureau of Labor Statistics. (2020, December 2). *Occupational Outlook Handbook*. U.S. Department of Labor. https://www.bls.gov/ooh/

MY OWN NOTES AND REFLECTIONS
ON CHAPTER 11

Describe the economy in the immediate area and region where you wish to work in or are currently working in. Given your professional job and career preferences, how healthy is the job market in those areas of interest? Make sure and have data to support your impression of the job market.

What are the data and policy organizations in your region that are similar to SANDAG in the San Diego region? What do professional experts say about the outlook for jobs and what are strategies for employment?

_____

_____

_____

_____

_____

_____

_____

_____

_____

_____

_____

_____

_____

_____

_____

_____

_____

_____

CHAPTER 12

FINDING ASSISTANCE WITH FINANCIAL, HEALTH, AND OTHER RESOURCE NEEDS

F inancial issues are among the top reasons why couples divorce. Married or not, I am sure you have experienced financial challenges and have seen how that type of worry not only affects your stress and anxiety levels but also how it influences your relationship to others. It also impacts your self-confidence and how you present yourself to others. Some individuals are better able to hide their stress, but most of us cannot. I remember being without a job and income for a few months when I was first starting a family and had young children and a wife who depended on me for income. I remember how stressful that was and how I got angry at my spouse for not helping financially by getting a job. It was not her fault we were in difficult situation. The financial stress caused me to use her as a scapegoat, blaming the closest person to me at the time. She also did the same, blaming me for not being a good provider and not being willing to take just any job to pay the rent and bring in food because I was waiting for my past employer to hire me again. It took two months to finally be employed, but the experience has stayed with me to this day.

Some of you may experience the same stress and anxiety that comes from problems with finances, perhaps because you or a loved one lost their job or because you find you are spending more for childcare or for your education. The first thing I recommend is that you plan as early as possible for financial problems. Seek out help and advice from community and government agencies. Here are some agencies and offices that can help you and inform you of available assistance at different governmental levels, including federal, state, and county.

Federal Government:

- Most of the federal assistance programs and funding are funneled through the state. For example, the Supplemental Nutrition Assistance Program (SNAP) provides healthy food for needy individuals and families. By looking at state and county websites, you will see what federally funded programs are available, like SNAP:

- URL: https://www.fns.usda.gov/snap/supplemental-nutrition-assistance-program

You may not live in California, but this gives you a sense of what is available to you from your state:
California State:

- California CalWORKS (Program provides financial assistance to needy individuals and families)
  - URL: https://www.benefits.gov/benefit/1229
- Employment Development Department, State of California (listing of additional practical resources, including help with food)
  - URL: https://www.edd.ca.gov/about_edd/Additional_Resources.htm

Stress and anxiety can lead to negative health issues, which can lead to indebtedness and further financial burden. Similarly, here is an example of what is available from the county of San Diego in the area of health, which should be similar to what you can find in your state and region:
San Diego County:

- Health and Human Services Agency (listing of links that include state and other government agency relief)
  - URL: https://www.sandiegocounty.gov/content/sdc/hhsa/programs/ssp/access/access_assistance_programs.html
- Specific for qualifying for Medi-Cal (provides information on applying for government medical insurance)
  - URL: https://www.sandiegocounty.gov/content/sdc/hhsa/programs/ssp/medi-cal_program/eligibility.html

Finally, you can often find help from your city or municipality. Here is an example of what can be found in San Diego, which you are likely to find in your municipality.
City of San Diego:

- COVID-19 Information and Resources (Contains a listing of various sources of help that include financial assistance. Other cities have similar lists.)
  - URL: https://www.sandiego.gov/citycouncil/cd9/covid19/resources

Regional and local community agencies can help connect you with food and financial assistance programs as well. Here are examples of some prominent organizations that provide such information in San Diego County, which would be similar to what you would find in your own county. Your county social services or health department offices can also be good places to get referrals for nonprofit organizations similar to those listed below in San Diego County.

- North County Health Services (Provides primarily health services but also provides helpful information and sometimes has non-health related programs that are helpful. Located throughout North County, including San Marcos, Oceanside, and Escondido.)
  - URL: https://www.nchs-health.org/community-resources/food-resources/
- Vista Community Clinic (Provides primarily health services and provides mental health services that are very helpful)
  - URL: http://www.vistacommunityclinic.org/health-services/behavioral-health/

When you locate the particular nonprofit organizations in your area that can help you with food, housing, financial assistance, and health services, visit their websites and look for a listing of programs and resources to find out what specific assistance they provide, including health care services.

Here are examples of additional community agencies in the San Diego area that can help with various health, mental health, food, counseling, case management, substance abuse, and job training services. Find the list of those similar organizations in your particular region.

- North County Lifeline, Oceanside (provides food assistance, job referral, vocational programming, parenting assistance, housing, counseling, child abuse, domestic violence, prevention/intervention programming, human trafficking prevention/intervention)
  - URL: https://www.nclifeline.org/communities-in-action
- Interfaith Community Services in Escondido (provides housing, job training, substance abuse, mental health, and other support services)
  - URL: https://www.interfaithservices.org/
- Center for Community Solutions in Escondido (provides legal assistance, short- and long-term shelter, counseling, domestic violence assistance, and a hotline)
  - URL: https://www.ccssd.org/
- North County Community Services, in San Marcos and Oceanside (Early childhood education)
  - URL: https://www.sdnccs.org/

- Community Resource Center in Encinitas (case management, provides food, shelter, counseling, and help with domestic violence)
    - URL: https://crcncc.org/
- Community Interface Services, in Carlsbad and San Diego (provides job/ vocational training, financial management counseling, independent living, and disability assistance programs)
    - URL: http://www.communityinterfaceservices.org/
- Women's Resource Center in Oceanside (provides domestic violence assistance, counseling, legal assistance, hotline, housing assistance, teen education programs)
    - URL: https://www.wrcsd.org/services/community-outreach

Counseling, Domestic or Intimate Partner Violence, and Suicide Prevention

Information is power, hope, and peace of mind. Use community and regional agencies and services—private or public—to help you with intimate partner violence or family conflict. Sometimes, good people with the best of intentions fall victim to interpersonal conflict and violence. Do not fall victim to victimization or perpetration that you may later regret, be it fighting, staying angry, scapegoating, losing hope, or attempting suicide. Sometimes financial, employment, or relationship problems lead people to become angry and the anger turns to conflict, at times ending with violence—verbal and physical. According to a survey conducted in August 2020 by the Centers for Disease Control and Prevention, 40% of American adults indicated grappling with at least one mental health or drug-related problem during the COVID-19 pandemic.[1] However, that number increased to 75% for young adults ages 18 to 24! The same survey showed that 25.5% of young adults 18 to 25 said they seriously considered suicide in the past 30 days, compared to 10.7% in 2018. Just so that you know, the vast majority of individuals who have survived jumping off bridges, such as from the Golden Gate Bridge, in an attempt to commit suicide report that they regret having jumped and never attempt to commit suicide again.[2] That tells you that moments of distress, while real and devastating, are temporary.

Mental illness, substance use, and suicidal ideation are all serious health problems facing young adults, which includes your age group. Please be sure not to ignore concerns you may have regarding any of these conditions and seek professional help. Therapists and counselors are much more available now than they were before the pandemic since therapy sessions are now done remotely and virtually—with good results. Your county or state health departments have behavioral health divisions that are able to either help you directly or refer you out if you do not have health insurance that covers these services. Also, you should call a hotline or 911 on behalf of others if you think they are at risk for hurting themselves or others. Calling 911 will connect you with dispatchers who have good referral sources for when time is of the essence.

Besides emergency calls to 911, there are national and local numbers that you can call in your area that can help you or someone near and dear to you. In regard to suicide, the National Suicide Hotline can help 24 hours a day, seven days a week: 1-800-273-8255. Here are agencies that can be contacted for those living in the San Diego region. They serve as examples of the types of organizations that possibly exist in your state and region that you can look for:

San Diego Access and Crisis Line	888-724-7240
Teen Suicide Prevention Hotline	760-509-3334
Women's Resource Center Crisis Hotline	760-757-3500

Accepting Low Paying or Even Nonpaid Positions

As mentioned earlier in the manual, during the Great Recession, many found it challenging to find professional jobs that were in line with their education or even with their training or past work experience. Individuals with master's or even PhD degrees were commonly seen standing in line in 2009 for any opportunities to get even a nonpaid internship or volunteer experience, thinking that it would either give them a foot in the door to the organization or would give them the experience and networking opportunities necessary to increase their chances of getting a paid job elsewhere. You may find yourself in the same situation if we end up living through a serious recession. If that happens, do avail yourself of any opportunities to gain experience that gives you that proverbial foot in the door to organizations or agencies that you are interested in, but also look at nonprofessional jobs that simply provide you with an income. Working at Costco, Trader Joes, or Starbucks are some good choices because they offer some employment and health benefits. You may need to be willing to take retail jobs as you wait for the economy to improve. Whatever you do, make sure to translate those "non-professional" experiences into professional job skills, training, and knowledge, making them relevant to future, more professional positions.

I remember one student who indicated having a hard time putting together a resume for a professional job that required a BA. She said, "What do I put down on my resume to get a professional job if all I've done is be a waitress?!" I then helped the student see that being a waitress provides a lot of skills that employers hiring for professional jobs look for in college-educated applicants. For example, a food server learns or demonstrates skills in many areas, including:

- Interpersonal relationships
- Communication
- Problem solving
- Handling conflict
- Working with others and in small groups
- Scheduling and planning
- Finances and accounting
- Working with diverse populations, including different age groups

In the same way, if you find yourself in a nonprofessional job, list out the professional skills you are gaining so that you are ready to share it with a future panel of interviewers.

This chapter focused on helping you become cognizant of available resources in your area and state that can assist you with common challenges that young college-educated adults have during serious recessions. Sometimes we refuse to seek out assistance because of our nature or pride. I hope this chapter encourages you to seek out assistance that can help meet your basic needs and thus reduce your stress and anxiety. Examples were provided from the San Diego area of services you are likely to find in your state and region. Use the examples to create a list of available helping organizations and government offices in your region that you can contact should you need help with your finances, housing, food, stress, anxiety, and other health needs. Finally, if jobs become as scarce as they did during the Great Recession, do not be afraid of taking jobs that do not require your college degree, but make sure that you convert all that you do into training, skills, knowledge, and experience that are needed in the professional jobs you will apply for once the recession subsides.

Notes

1. Czeisler, M. E., Lane, R. I., Petrosky, E., Wiley, J. F., Christensen, A., Njai, R., Weaver, M. D., Robbins, R., Faucer-Childs, E. R., Barger, L. K., Cseisler, C. A., Howard, M. E., & Rajaratnam, S. M. W. (2020). *Mental health, substance abuse, and suicidal ideation during the COVID-19 pandemic—United States, June 24–30, 2020* (Morbidity and Mortality Weekly Report 2020; 69). Centers for Disease Control and Prevention.
2. Newman, E. (2019, February 20). *A lesson from 29 Golden Gate suicide attempts.* Medium. https://ennyman.medium.com/a-lesson-from-29-golden-gate-suicide-attempts-a42f4ef3f970

MY OWN NOTES AND REFLECTIONS ON CHAPTER 12

Questions and activities to consider, besides your own notes.

Describe your current financial standing. Specify areas of specific need tied to finances, housing, food, childcare (if relevant), health, and mental health and devise a plan for meeting those needs. Develop a list of organizations or government agencies in your state and region, with their contact numbers, that you can contact to help you in the various areas in which you need help. Develop a list of confidants, such as friends and family members, who you can talk to about problems you have in any area to get their support, assistance, counseling, and feedback regarding any plans you develop.

_____

_____

_____

_____

_____

_____

_____

_____

_____

_____

_____

_____

_____

_____

_____

_____

_____

_____

_____

_____

CHAPTER 13

IT'S OKAY TO NOT HAVE A CAREER PASSION

One of the greatest fallacies we have as humans is the belief that deep down inside each of us we have a passion or career that we were destined or meant to pursue and all we need do is to get that sucker out of us somehow! Parents and older relatives forget—or sometimes wish to forget—what it was like for them when they were your age and trying to figure out what their calling was or decide which career to pursue. Because they love you, parents or guardians have very high expectations for their children. If you are a first-generation college student, the pressure is even worse since parents who did not get a college education expect that you will avoid *all* the financial and resource needs and hardships they went through by getting that college degree. The questions they often ask add to your stress and sense of failure, particularly during a recession. They might say "What career or job will you get with your degree?" or "Why did you graduate with a degree that does not assure you of a good paying job?" First, what you need to know is that NO ONE has a secret innate drive for a particular job or career. The truth is that we develop our passions for careers or jobs based on experiences we gain in the world and in various fields, be it through jobs or volunteer experiences or by being in a positive work environment with great supervisors or bosses who encourage you and tell you of opportunities you can choose.

Watch this video by Terri Trespicio where she suggests that you should stop searching for your passion:

https://www.youtube.com/watch?v=6MBaFL7sCb8

Then watch this video by Celeste Headlee suggesting that you stop trying to find a job but rather a mission:

https://www.youtube.com/watch?v=VVx6ntr5OqI

Having said this, I also have to recognize that it is true that some people really do know early in life what they wish to do and actually do it successfully later in life as a career. I am thinking of Jim Carey, the actor, who knew early on that he wanted to be a comedian. His father also knew from a young age that he wanted to be a comedian, but he felt he could not follow that passion so he became a frustrated accountant in order to support his family. The worst thing is that his father's sacrifice was in vain, since he ended up losing his accounting job. In reality, most people do not know what career they want even as they are graduating with their college degree. They may feel they know what they *should* do, but knowing for sure what they should do is something different. So, if I am right about the fact that most people do not have a clear passion that will lead them to their dream job, then, I say, stop trying to chase this unlikely situation. Instead, step out into life with your recently earned degree, go through the first door (or job) that grabs your interest, and watch as other doors open up, just waiting for you to walk through them. Eventually, you will be doing that which you will at some point recognize as fitting your internal passion or, more realistically, your passions (plural). Tell yourself and your family, who might pressure you to reveal your occupational passions and plan for immediately earnings, that they need to trust you to make decisions based on opportunities and interests you currently have. Your college degree will be key to you entering a professional world, even if at the present time you are gaining basic job skills and the experience necessary for succeeding as a professional. Inform them that in all likelihood you will eventually be earning significantly more than if you did not attain your college degree.

By the way, I do suggest that you watch Jim Carey's graduation commencement speech he gave because it is very inspirational (https://www.youtube.com/watch?v=V80-gPkpH6M).

Another commencement speech by an actor to watch, if you have not seen it already, is Matthew McConaughey's commencement speech where he presents five principles to live by (https://www.youtube.com/watch?v=BmCTQ_mkzHU).

In Life, You Will Fail

This subtitle sounds depressing and out of place, but it is important, if not critical, for you to consider and understand. Every human being experiences failure (be it failing a class, getting fired or demoted, failing to live up to parental expectations or those of your friends, partners, etc.). Albert Einstein dropped out of school and failed his college entrance exam. Failing is part of life. You need to get over it if your failures are affecting your self-concept or self-esteem. What is *not* part of a healthy life or experience is *purposely* failing or doing things that you *know* will lead you to self-harm or to harming others, such as falling victim to alcohol or drug addiction.

Live life in such a way that you savor the beauty of each day by appreciating what you have—not focusing on what you do not have or what others have that you do not have. Rather, you should appreciate all the things that you have and who you are (e.g., having relatively good health and the ability to see, smell, hear, talk, think, feel, laugh, cry, yell, love, etc.). Focus on all those things, characteristics, abilities, and knowledge that you have that makes you a unique and fortunate person and then be appreciative. List these out in writing and put the list where you can see it so that when you are consumed by a problem or worries, you will see it and it will make you feel better.

Be a Giver to Others

This concept is not only biblical but is also an undeniable truth: To give is to receive. A giver often receives more than what they give. Regardless of your degree, the attitude that you have when working is critical for your happiness and appreciation for your job and life. Develop or reinforce an attitude of serving others, of meeting needs or of solving problems. Have an attitude of giving and not of expecting to receive. This is not to say that you should not expect what is right and just, including being paid fairly. However, those who have a positive attitude of giving or serving are happier, and others, like employers, tend to appreciate them and reward them with new or enhanced opportunities. When presented with a job or career choice, ask yourself which choice will feed that natural part of you that makes you feel the most satisfied and will mutually benefit your talents, experience, and education. Attitude is everything. Having a giving or serving attitude will impress others and fulfill the innate human drive to serve others.

This chapter has tried to demonstrate the fact that, as humans, we all have many interests and talents that can fit a variety of professional careers. Some of us have been exposed to or influenced to go into particular careers, which then makes it easier to know which degree to attain. However, for many, career choice is not easily discernable. Many of my graduating seniors still wonder what they will do with their degrees. My message to these students and to you is that it is okay to not know for sure what your career should be. What is important is that you be informed of the job and career choices that are available with your degree and that you start making some decisions. By working at any job, you will learn how interested you are in particular activities, such as helping customers/clients or documenting/developing programs. Learn from the experiences and advice of others, such as those presented to you in the chapter. Know that we all fail at one time or another. Failures do not destroy us but rather allow us to learn and gain wisdom. Albert Einstein could have given up on science when he failed the college entrance exam, but thankfully, he continued with his felt interest in the field of science. He clearly had a positive attitude toward his interest. Finally, make sure and heed the call to develop a positive and giving attitude since such attitudes will help you to be truly happy in what you eventually do as a career and in life.

MY OWN NOTES AND REFLECTIONS
ON CHAPTER 13

Do you have a passion for a particular field or career? If so, write it out and describe your passion and interest. If you do not have a passion, are you bothered by not having one?

After watching the recommended videos, do you now feel less pressure to have a single passion? Describe those things you see yourself doing in a profession or with particular populations who you wish to work with that make you happy.

Do you feel pressure to be perfect and not fail? If so, develop a plan for reducing that pressure.

Do you have a giving attitude or interest in serving others? If not, develop a plan for how your career interests can be a part of an attitude of serving or helping others.

_____

_____

_____

_____

_____

_____

_____

_____

_____

_____

_____

_____

_____

_____

_____

CHAPTER 14

DEVELOP AN ACTION PLAN

A s mentioned in the previous chapter, you do not have to have a passion that dictates what to do in life in terms of a career. You only need enough information about career choices and options to choose from when considering starting your professional life using your degree. Any field experience, volunteer opportunity, or job will likely provide you with knowledge of things you like doing and populations with which you enjoy working. Use that knowledge gained to date, add to it new knowledge you have about available career options, and use that information to develop a career action plan. During major economic downturns or recessions, your job or career choices may be limited, but you need to remember that you *always* have options. I recommend that you get a notebook to use for only job and career planning. Begin by listing your short- and long-term career or job goals or interests. You do not have to be 100% sure or committed to these options, but noting them will give you something to refer to while planning. Your commitment to each career or job listed can range from highly committed to "I'm not sure, but I think these are my short- and long-term career or job seeking goals." Indicate your level of commitment to each choice, note the reasons why, and add counterarguments so that you clearly see the positives and negatives of each career option.

People with Specific Passions

If you find you are highly committed to a particular career or occupation, consider the current job market and whether you need to get a graduate degree to secure that occupation. List steps you feel that you need to take to get from where you are now to obtaining that desired job or career or entry into a graduate program. For example, if you are highly motivated and committed to using your degree to become a social worker or case manager despite knowing that many such professionals have been laid off due to the recession, you can develop a specialized strategy that takes into account the competitive nature of the position you are pursuing. Perhaps, you can focus on a particular employer that typically hires a lot of social workers within and outside your county, like Child Welfare or Child Protective Services. You can then develop a well-thought-out, specific plan for getting ahead of the line of those applying for any available positions. That plan can include the following steps:

1. Learn about the practice of social work within the particular organization. What do they do there? What populations do they work with? What are the common challenges faced by client populations? What problems do social workers face on the job? What skills, knowledge, experience, and training should social workers have?

2. Become knowledgeable in the subject areas outlined in Step 1. Read and conduct informational interviews with past or current social workers in the organization to not only become informed but also to become known by those in the organization.

3. Develop a plan for becoming known by those in the department or organization of interest. Offer to become a volunteer or intern.

4. Share your career or job plan with confidants or friends and listen to yourself as you present your plan to network with those in the organization(s) you are interested in developing a relationship with.

5. Activate your plan by meeting or, at the very least, communicating directly with those in the targeted organization(s). Try to do this with more than one agency or organization to increase the chances of success. After doing so, share your experience with your confidants or significant others to further encourage you and to elicit feedback and advice on next steps.

What you need to know is that even during a severe recession or in a tight job market, there is always job turnover and available slots that will need to be filled. You can be the next replacement worker if you become known through your outreach efforts. Employers always prefer to hire those who they know of and who are passionate about their organization, even if they may not be the most qualified!

People Without Specific Passions

If you do not have a strong passion for a specific career or job, you likely have various interests. That is just as fine as having a clear focus or passion for a particular field. The advantage of not being committed to any one field is that you can respond to a variety of job or career opportunities as they emerge. You should still use a notebook to note the various options that appeal to you and that you feel are viable and realistic for you. Rank options by either interest or accessibility (i.e., low to high interest, hard to easier to get). It is important that you then share that list with trusted individuals. Doing so will allow you to think through the options. As mentioned before, we often learn from listening to ourselves argue for various options. In doing so we often discover passions we may not have noticed. Moreover, talking to others will provide you with advice and feedback on your choices. For those who know what career or job they want, develop a list of steps to follow similar to those suggested above for people who don't know what they want. Know that you will still need to take action to use your degree. Out of the various employment possibilities, choose one to three places you wish to apply to. Learn all you can about the organizations of interest and try to make contact with them, as indicated above. Your experience doing this will help you know how excited you are about various job options.

The focus of this chapter was to encourage you to develop a plan of action that lists out the steps you should take. It is not enough to know about career or job options. You will need to take action. Breaking down a plan into steps helps you to know how to start the process. If you know what you wish to do with your degree, you have a focus that can direct you to specific employers you may be interested in working for. If you do not have a career focus, you have more options to consider, which you can rank, choosing up to three to focus on in developing your plan of action. Always talk to confidants and share your plans with them and practice what you plan on saying to people you want to talk to in organizations of interest. This will help you listen to yourself as you argue for a plan with specific steps. Think about developing short- and long-term goals or plans.

MY OWN NOTES AND REFLECTIONS
ON CHAPTER 14

Have you developed a specific plan for what you will do now that you have graduated? If so, does it have specific steps to follow? If not, develop a plan that describes specific steps you will take to find and secure a professional job or specific occupation, or simply a job to pay the bills. Develop short- and long-term plans that include specific steps you will take to achieve these goals.

_____

_____

_____

_____

_____

_____

_____

_____

_____

_____

_____

_____

_____

_____

_____

_____

_____

_____

_____

_____

_____

CHAPTER 15

CONSIDER MOVING, EVEN IF ONLY TEMPORARILY

Going Where the Jobs Are

I remember when I was living in San Diego working as a doctoral student for the U.S. Navy as a researcher. I was almost finished with my PhD and was barely making it financially because, like for many today, the cost of living was higher than my paycheck. I had to take care of my two young children and wife who stayed home with them. If I found a penny on the floor, I did not consider it a lucky penny but, instead, a necessary one to collect. Every penny was critical. When any raise was given to federal employees, our landlord somehow knew of it and would immediately raise our rent by the exact amount of my raise, so we never made any headway financially. It was really so very stressful. Upon finishing my doctorate, my mentor at the University of Colorado, where I got my PhD, told me to consider doing the same thing he did when he was in my situation after graduating with his PhD. He said to move out of the state and go to the Midwest where the cost of living is much lower and where you will be more needed and appreciated, at least compared to the states on each coast where you have many more people vying for the same positions.

I followed his advice and accepted my first academic job at the University of Missouri, Kansas City. Making almost the same income there as I had in San Diego allowed me to buy a four-bedroom home with a humongous yard, two-car garage, and basement thanks to the much lower cost of living. My children were so happy to have so much space. The other thing I found was that, unlike in Southern California, neighbors really wanted to get to know you and establish a relationship with you and your family. For the first time, I felt I had enough money to spend on what we needed. Eventually, I left and came back to California, after having built my career and increased my experience as a successful academic and researcher. If you find that you cannot make headway financially where you are, you should consider moving to where there are more jobs and less people competing for them and where the cost of living and housing is less—at least temporarily. Sometimes, particular jobs and careers in certain regions of the country dry up but flourish in other areas. I know that it is tough and challenging to move, but just know this is sometimes a good thing to do to get your career started or to make sure you have an adequate income to live on, reducing stress caused by finances. Keep in mind that moving does not mean you will never come back to your place of origin or preference. You can plan to return after a couple of years or so. At least think about this as an option. Having such options reduces stress levels because it makes you feel you are not up against the wall with no solutions to your employment and financial problems.

Going Where Family Is

For some, the option is not to leave from being around family but going to where family is to support you. For example, you may have parents or relatives in other parts of the state or outside of the state. These family members may have temporary housing and/or may be able to provide you with material and financial support. In fact, many choose to live with relatives, such as parents, during recessions with high unemployment. If you do that, develop a specific plan that lists the support you expect to get for a specified timeframe so that you do not simply go without a plan or calendar. That will help ensure you don't "float" endlessly and will convey to your family that you only need some temporary help instead of planning on being an indefinite burden. That will give everyone peace of mind, creating a more positive atmosphere that will lead to a greater likelihood of others lending support.

Going Where the Cost of Living Is Less

It is always easier to get your career going in locations where the cost of living is less than where it is high. I really do not know how young professionals make it where I live, in San Diego County. Housing is expensive, cost of living is high, and education like graduate programs are expensive and competitive. In considering your career plan, think of moving to places where the cost of living is low and where there are growing opportunities in the fields of interest to you. If you move out of the area to another part of the country, you will be learning how America is culturally diverse, full of various cultures you never knew existed that have nothing to do with immigrants or ethnic minority groups or cultures. The Midwest and the South have their own unique cultures, foods, practices, celebrations, and accents just like we do here in Southern California. When I was in Boulder Colorado, everyone had to be a Broncos fan, and in Boulder, you rooted for the Colorado Buffs—no choice. You cannot be just a regular casual fan. During the Broncos football season, you have to be a crazy, orange-painted, Christmas-tree-loving fan with an orange-colored wardrobe and all! You learn about regional differences that will later help you to work with more diverse populations wherever you end up settling.

This chapter presented arguments for why if you are struggling financially or are having problems finding employment in your current location, you, having recently gained your college degree, should possibly consider moving out of your current location and preferred permanent location—at least temporarily. An article in *USA Today* reported that more than 10% of Americans move each year due mainly to marriage or economic reasons, such as obtaining a new job.[1] Major recessions offer incentives to move due to better employment markets or lower cost of living in other parts of the country. Many decide to move in with family in other parts of the country as a way of establishing themselves career-wise and economically. Even if economic problems are not a factor, I still encourage my students to consider temporarily moving to another part of the country to broaden their experience. If you are planning to go to graduate school, choose to go to a large research university since they are likely to offer you subsidized housing, greater financial aid, and the possibility of good employment on campus. I say more about this in the next chapter, which covers graduate degrees.

Note

1. Suneson, G. (2020, August 4). Lack of jobs is among the top reason Americans are exiting these cities across the U.S. *USA Today*. https://www.usatoday.com/story/money/2020/08/04/cities-americans-are-abandoning-for-new-jobs-careers/112604384/

MY OWN NOTES AND REFLECTIONS ON CHAPTER 15

Questions and activities to consider, besides your own notes.

Describe the opportunities or lack thereof where you live or prefer to work currently. Does it offer opportunities for you to secure a job and launch your career? If not, how likely are you to consider moving to a place that offers more professional opportunities and/or a lower cost of living?

If you find it challenging to find a job or to afford housing where you are now, list out the pros and cons for temporarily moving to another location that does offer more opportunities. Do research and identify places to move to in other parts of the state or country that may help you launch your professional career.

_____

_____

_____

_____

_____

_____

_____

_____

_____

_____

_____

_____

_____

_____

_____

_____

_____

_____

_____

_____

CHAPTER 16

IMPORTANCE OF A GRADUATE DEGREE

You have heard it said before, perhaps by a peer, "A BA or BS degree is now the high school diploma of the past—everyone has one!" That sentiment causes you to feel bad about the degree you worked so hard to get or pressures you to consider going into graduate school, or both. As mentioned previously, only about one third of the adult population in the United States have a bachelor's degree. That makes you part of an elite and special group of people that employers look to for higher level assistance that someone with only a high school degree cannot offer. Employers know that college-educated students are better able to help come up with solutions to problems or give them wise advice, thereby helping them achieve their organizational goals. Why? Because college students have been exposed through their classes to historical, contemporary, and future problems at various levels, such as scientific, biological, sociological, psychological, and literary. Certainly, college provides more in-depth coverage on these topics than high school does.

Perhaps you feel the pressure to get a graduate degree because you do not have those around you who know the value of an undergraduate degree. You may be a first-generation college student who does not have college-educated parents who know firsthand how special and marketable you are with BA degree. Even college-educated parents sometimes do not know the value of an undergraduate degree like a BA or BS. They themselves may minimize its value since they do not know how to leverage such a degree with employers. Having said that, for some people, pursuing a graduate degree may indeed be a wise thing to do, but for others it may be foolish. Let us consider why this is so.

Risks of Getting a Graduate Degree

Getting a graduate degree, like an MA or MS or even a doctorate, means that you, in theory, are worth more because you have more training and education. Keep in mind that during a recession, employers are also hurting financially and they usually tend to not hire people with graduate degrees because applicants with such degrees expect to earn more and/or expect to get promoted faster, thus increasing the pressure on employers to pay more for that person's expertise. During the Great Recession of 2007–2009, many who had graduate degrees hid that fact in their job applications to avoid being disqualified from jobs because they were considered overqualified or because the organization would have to pay them more. School districts are in that situation. They have formulas they use to determine the rate of pay. The greater the number of college course units, the more they need to pay you. However, during recessions or economic downturns school budgets tend to be lower due to lower tax revenues. As a result, they will overlook you if you have a graduate degree or too many college units.

Benefits of Pursuing a Graduate Degree

There are some reasons why it may be beneficial to pursue a graduate degree during a recession. During the Great Recession, some college graduates decided that they wanted to wait it out by getting a graduate degree. They figured, "Why not use student loans or fellowships to pay for my housing and living expenses while I am also getting a graduate degree that increases my chances of getting a good paying job? I can then better plan for what to do with my degree when the recession subsides." The other possible advantage is that if you go to a large research university, they likely will have subsidized housing that is a fraction of the cost of off-campus housing. I lived in such an apartment in Boulder, Colorado, when I was a graduate student there. I paid a fraction of the cost of housing that was available outside the university, and it enabled me to not need a car since everything was on or near campus (e.g., food, entertainment, shopping, etc.). As a matter of fact, I remember thinking after I got my first "professional" paycheck after moving away from the university, "Dang! I was relatively rich as a student compared to now with my professional paycheck that does not cover much of the cost of housing and cost of living!" If you are married and/or have children and decide to get a graduate degree, get it from a large research university—you cannot find a more supportive, economically viable, pleasant, enjoyable, and supportive environment for you and your children.

As a student at CU Boulder, we lived in family housing with other young families. Families there supported one another. Student families had developed a token-based system of helping with childcare. You paid something like $50 dollars and you were given something like 20 tokens, each worth one hour of babysitting, and a list of other students with children who were willing to babysit in order to gain tokens so that they too could have sitters take care of their own children. Essentially, the system enabled us to have free childcare! Plus, you had the added advantage of making friends with other parents who also shared their knowledge of parenting and child development. These friends who were parents themselves would also tell you about child-friendly entertainment options. Also, the formal childcare centers at the university were available to students at a substantially reduced cost. For those who have school-age children, the schools surrounding most universities are among the best schools in the nation. They are usually staffed by university graduates who want to provide or implement the most innovative curriculum and education possible.

Beyond childcare, schools, and housing, research universities, called R1 universities because of their primary focus on research, are special because they grant doctorates and generate lots of money through research grants and from endowments, usually from alumni or companies. State universities are not "Research 1" or "R1" universities but rather are *teaching universities*, meaning that the faculty's primary focus is on teaching the students as opposed to research, even if most do conduct research and publish regularly. They typically do not grant doctorates but only master's and bachelor's degrees. They may have one or two doctoral programs but they usually work with R1 universities to grant these. Faculty at these teaching universities do get research grants, but the pressure on faculty to have them is not as great as those faculty in R1 universities. Therefore, teaching universities do not benefit as much from the revenue that comes from research grants.

Just so that you know, when universities get federal grants for research, they get extra overhead money from the federal government to pay for infrastructure and student aid through what is called an *indirect rate* that is determined by the federal government. These federally negotiated rates are typically over 60%. That means that if I get a research grant for $100,000, the university will get an extra $60,000 to help pay for the university's infrastructure, or 60% over the awarded grant amount. Typically, the larger and more committed a university is to conducting research, the larger the indirect rate, often over 75%. So, you can see that research universities that get over one billion dollars in research grants get almost the same amount for their infrastructure. A university uses those funds for their infrastructure of the university (e.g., buildings, facilities, and upkeep), but they can also use those funds to pay for student stipends, fellowships, grants, or even student assistantships. Therefore, another advantage of going to a research university is that you often find a significant amount of employment there on campus.

You Decide What Is Right for You

Bottom line, when considering getting a graduate degree during a recession, you need to plan well and know what your priorities and goals are. Do you want to continue to be in school or do you want to start working? That is the choice you need to make. Just make sure not to minimize the importance and value of your degree, whatever you do. Do not consider it to be on par with getting a high school diploma—*it is not.* If you decide on a graduate program, know the advantages and disadvantages of doing so.

Financial and Debt Considerations

If you decide to go to graduate school, you should not go to an expensive school and get into debt. Minimize your student loans because they will follow you almost to your grave! That is why a research university is a good choice and a public one is best. If you are worried about paying expensive out-of-state tuition, just know it will only be for the first year, and some graduate programs even pay the difference in tuition for that first year. After the first year, you can apply to be a resident of the state, thereby qualifying for in-state tuition. Before selecting a graduate school, look into the university fellowships, scholarships, and grants that they provide. The department you are interested in typically can give you information about special financial aid available through the department or university. Financial aid offices can also tell you about different sources of federal and state aid. You can also ask about paid teaching assistantships, where you help professors grade their student's work or assist in their classes. That has the added advantage of giving you teaching experience.

Graduate School Experience

I just want to remind you of what was said earlier; the experience of graduate school is very different than the undergraduate experience. In graduate school, you will be asked to think more and come up with solutions to problems or get a higher level of understanding on topics based on current knowledge and research (i.e., critical thinking). As a result, you will read more and share your analysis of readings in class. Classes are smaller and more intimate. You cannot hide in a typical graduate seminary class. Professors and peers will know if you did your assigned readings or not.

The purpose of this chapter was to inform you of the advantages and disadvantages of getting a graduate degree. You need to be sure you want that degree and carefully plan what you will do with it. Consider its cost and what you will be paid in a job requiring that degree. If you decide to get a graduate degree, plan it out well and talk to current students in the graduate program you are considering attending to get their opinions on the benefits and disadvantages of the program. Always be willing to communicate with past professors to get their opinion about the school and graduate program you are considering. Consider talking to professors from the graduate program you are considering. Read their online biographies before contacting them so that you get to know them. Reading biographies of faculty will also tell you about specialties within the graduate program. Get feedback and information from as many people as possible to give you enough information to make the wisest decision. Finally, make sure to look at financial aid available through the graduate program, their department, or through the university. Also, look for financial aid in the form of scholarships, fellowships, and grants through broader sources. You can find this information in the books at your university's library or online.

MY OWN NOTES AND REFLECTIONS ON CHAPTER 16

Questions and activities to consider, besides your own notes.

What arguments in this chapter regarding pros and cons of getting a graduate degree caught your attention, and why?

To what extent do you wish to pursue a graduate degree? If you do want to pursue a graduate degree, what degree is it and what jobs do you see yourself using it for? Find out the pay ranges for the career(s) you will use a graduate degree for and determine if it is satisfactory for you. Write out the pros and cons of securing a graduate degree for yourself.

If you are planning for a graduate degree, identify graduate programs that offer the most in terms of financial aid and that cost the least in terms of tuition, housing, and cost of living. If you decide to get a graduate degree, make a plan to talk to professors and students from the graduate programs of interest.

_____

_____

_____

_____

_____

_____

_____

_____

_____

_____

_____

_____

_____

_____

_____

_____

_____

CHAPTER 17

JOBS AVAILABLE WITH JUST A BACHELOR'S DEGREE

A s mentioned earlier, you need to appreciate the value of your under-graduate degree and not look down on it. I know devaluing your degree will be a temptation for you when you are finding it difficult to find a job, but that does not minimize the value of your degree. Your degree qualifies you for many professional jobs that pay well. I will point out some jobs that you may not know that you qualify for with only your BA or BS.

Science and Technology

Much of the information provided here comes from the *Occupational Outlook Handbook* that is published by the U.S. Department of Labor.[1] Currently, there is a significant growth in jobs in the sciences, be it tied to computers, health, or education. Let me give you a few examples of such jobs. Those graduating with a BS in biology can qualify for biological technician jobs that pay the median income of $45,000 annually, or $22 hourly. In the *Occupational Outlook Handbook*, you will also see bachelor's-level positions that pay a median salary ranging from $45,000 to $75,000. These include clinical laboratory technologists and technicians, forensic science technicians, microbiologists, zoologists, and wildlife biologists. In the computer and information technology sector, you can find bachelor's-level jobs that pay a higher median annual salary ranging from $55,000 to $113,000. These positions include computer network architects, computer programmers, computer support specialists, computer systems analysts, database administrators, information security analysts, network and computer systems administrators, software developers, and web developers. Engineers in various areas can expect to get paid more with their BS degrees in engineering, with median annual salaries starting at $53,000.

Social and Behavioral Sciences and Human Services

The occupational handbook mentioned earlier also lists various occupations requiring only a BA or BS related to human services in one way or another. The median annual salary will generally range from $46,000 to $67,000. You will see such occupations listed as probation officers and correctional treatment specialists; health educators and community health workers; substance abuse, behavioral disorder, and mental health counselors; and social and community service managers.

Social Work and Case Management

Social work and case management are highlighted here because there are many jobs with this title throughout the United States, many are tied to government agencies, hospitals, schools, and not-for-profit organizations. Both terms are interchangeable, since they often refer to the same job or occupation. The field of social work is attractive to many students because the field is broad in its coverage, ranging from understanding systemic societal influences on humans to individual or psychological factors. However, in many states, including California, you do not need to have a degree in social work to have the title and job of a social worker. In theory, even people with seemingly unrelated degrees can become social workers. For example, students with a degree in Spanish or an Asian language, like Cambodian or Vietnamese, can secure a job as a social worker because their language skills may be in demand. Similarly, you can also become a social worker or case manager if you have received a BA in art or music if you demonstrate an interest in underserved or minority populations where there is a need for those with such expertise.

There are many social work programs at universities that grant degrees in social work, be it a Bachelor of Social Work (BSW) or a Master of Social Work (MSW). If you go through a social work program, you will learn about the importance of various social, educational, cultural, and societal contexts that influence or impact individuals. Such students learn about the micro and macro levels of influence on individuals. Beyond the jargon, interdisciplinary programs, like human development and other social science programs, also expose students to the same multilevel and interdisciplinary perspectives. In acknowledging these diverse influences on populations, social workers learn to try to address the needs of individuals and their families at different levels, which includes helping to secure housing, education, food/nutrition, training, and employment. In essence, case managers or social workers learn to be brokers of different types of available services that benefit clients. They become familiar with various services and programs in the community and of those offered by the government. Their goal is to link client needs with the services available to them. They do assessments to determine needs that they then use to find appropriate services for their clients. These are things that any social science or behavioral science graduate knows or can learn to do.

Most employers who are hiring for social worker positions will be just as happy to hire a person with a BA in any social science major, which includes human development or those with a BA who possess specialized skills, like being bilingual or experience working with underserved populations. As an example, San Diego County's Child Welfare Office routinely hires BA-degreed individuals without a social work degree. What they have told me is that they put more importance on hiring individuals with a BA who are able to work well with others and who understand culturally and socially diverse underserved populations. Being bilingual is a particularly important trait that is critical when working with linguistically diverse populations. Those interested in working as either social workers or case managers can look for such jobs in these places:

- child protective divisions (in San Diego County it is called child welfare)
- county departments of aging
- state departments of aging
- military base family and dependent service centers and programs
- community health centers
- community-based agencies
- hospitals and health system organizations, such as Kaiser Permanente and children's hospitals
- veteran's hospitals and programs for homeless vets
- homeless serving programs and agencies
- elementary and high schools (usually those that are large and in underserved communities)
- school district offices
- employment training agencies and programs
- regional centers that focus on disabled and special-education populations
- mental health offices and centers
- youth programs and organizations

It is common for community-based social or health service agencies to advertise hiring positions for *case managers*, not social workers, since managing cases is what a social worker does. Currently, California and other states do not offer title protection to the social-work label, and that is why many social workers in California and other states do not need to have either a BSW or MSW to have the social work title, which is considered more descriptive of their role. As you can imagine, there are many uses for professionals who help find available services for the populations in need of them. That is why there are so many jobs for case managers or social workers. Sometimes, these services brokers can also have additional titles, such as community service worker, community outreach worker, youth services worker, or family services worker. The common characteristic of social work positions is that their main job is to find services for particular underserved populations.

Teaching and Substituting

To teach in a public school, you will need to obtain a teaching credential, either at the primary or secondary level, meaning at the elementary, middle, or high school level. It typically takes about a year to get a credential. I highly recommend those getting a credential also get special education training, a special education certificate, or a special education credential at either the mild-to-moderate or moderate-to-severe levels. It will typically take only a few more months to get these add-ons to your credential, but it will mean you will be more highly prized as a teacher *even if you decide not to work directly with special education students*. With a special education credential, you will be more likely to be able to choose the district you want to work for; plus, you will get paid more.

Substitute Teaching

In California, like some other states, you do not need a teaching credential to substitute teach. You can substitute in classrooms with only your BA and earn about $100 per day. You will only need to pass the CBEST exam (California Basic Educational Skills Test),[2] which ensures that you have very basic reading, writing, and math skills. Most BA-degreed students pass the exam the first time with no problem. Other states have basic skills tests like the California CBEST. Others only require that you have a certain number of college units, like Missouri, Nevada, New Jersey, and Virginia. Check your particular state's requirements. You will find that substitute teaching can be an easy way of earning income with little preparation beyond your BA or BS.

Teaching Without a Credential

Some states allow bachelor's-level individuals to teach without a credential, special license, or certificate. For example, some states, like Texas, Missouri, Kentucky, Wisconsin, Mississippi, California, and Arizona, currently allow for emergency credential or licensure to teach in areas where there is a shortage of teachers in particular areas, such as in the sciences. In California, for example, individuals with only a BA or BS can teach in private schools as a teacher without a credential or certificate. This is allowed because no public funds are used for private school education. However, before applying for a teaching job at a private school, it is recommended that you take the CBEST or comparable basic knowledge test in your state exam as a way of demonstrating your basic educational competency, at least when seeking to teach at the primary- or elementary-school level. To teach at the middle- or high-school level, you will likely need to prove a specialty in the various single-subject areas, such as math, biology, English, a foreign language (if teaching a foreign language), social sciences/history, or sports/physical education. In California, one way of demonstrating single-subject specialty is for you to pass the California Educator Credentialing Examination (CSET)[3] in a particular area, such as in the social sciences and history. CSET in social sciences and history includes material on U.S. history, geography, economics, civics, and California history. I mention the social sciences and history specialty because it complements those majoring in and graduating with a social sciences degree, like human development. Something similar may be the case in other states. Check with the department of education for your state or ask someone in a school at which you would be interested in teaching. Do not forget to also ask about private schools since there might be different requirements to teach in such schools.

Health Services

As mentioned in an earlier chapter, the growth of jobs during the Great Recession of 2007–2009 were mainly in the health and education areas. The same is likely to happen with the (probable) upcoming recession. If you go online and find the U.S. Department of Labor's *Occupational Outlook Handbook*[4] and you did a search there using the term "health services," you will find certain occupations listed, such as medical and health services managers, community health educators, and substance abuse and behavioral disorder or mental health counselors. You are qualified for all these occupations with your social BA or BS and with any knowledge or experience gained on your own while working in health care settings or with diverse underserved populations. If you enter "education and health" in the *Occupational Outlook Handbook,* you will find information about occupations in the areas of educational services and health care and social assistance, which you might find of interest and qualify for with your undergraduate degree.

An online article by the job search website Monster on health care jobs points out that jobs in hospital or in-patient settings will likely be declining in favor of outpatient or home care services.[5] The COVID-19 crisis is contributing to this trend, causing health education and care to be increasingly delivered remotely, using mediums like Zoom and Skype or simply by using the phone. This is called *telemedicine*. Currently, most jobs in telemedicine are for doctors and other licensed specialists. However, you will start seeing a lot more jobs like this one at the University of Virginia for a "telemedicine client services associate" that does not require more than a BA and performs the following functions on behalf of the Office of Telemedicine:

- Supports the development of new [telemedicine] programs and the maintenance of current programs.
- Coordinates and maintains clinical operations for continuity and efficiency of services for our customers to include Clinic Preparation Clinic and On-Call Support Clinic Documentation and Review.
- Provides exceptional customer service in a manner to maximize satisfaction and loyalty of our customers including patients and internal and external partners and associates.
- Performs variety of operational and clerical duties to support department operations.
- Performs area-specific support activities for special projects or events.
- In addition to the above job responsibilities, other duties may be assigned.[6]

I predict that you will see a growing number of such nonlicensed jobs that support telemedicine and education. Keep your eye out for them or contact telemedicine offices to see what jobs they expect to have in providing remote client or patient support services. You will also see a growing number of jobs that support and educate patients, young and old, about their medical conditions and the support services available to them. Examples of these jobs include child life specialists, patient advocates, health care social workers, or health educators. All major health care providers know the importance of such professions since they prevent further illnesses or medical complications, which saves them money. Other fast-growing areas in health care include jobs in what is called health care analytics, which includes health data analysts. These jobs do not require more than a high school education, but they do desire experience with data, which most social or behavioral science major graduates have experience with. All such majors have to take classes in statistics and research methods. Human development and other interdisciplinary majors are also often required to take an applied research class where they gather, analyze, and report on data collected. That type of experience will qualify you for such data analyst jobs in health care.

Other in-demand jobs in health care include claims processors or representatives and medical insurance representatives. All health care providers need to have individuals verify or process insurance coverage or claims. Like health care data analysts, claims or insurance representatives are usually trained on the job because there are few individuals with such experience. The other available jobs are in health care customer service as representatives, or concierges. Finally, there is a growing need for hospital administrators and medical administrative assistants. These do have additional requirements for certificates and training, but the training is not overwhelming. Many universities, like ours (Cal State San Marcos), offer a 360-hour or 45-day medical assistant training certificate. Community colleges also offer similar courses and programs related to medical assistant or medical management as well. To become a medical assistant in California, you need to pass the Medical Assistants Examination offered by the California Certifying Board for Medical Assistants. The examination has three parts, but you only need to pass the basic exam to become certified. To get a job in a more administrative area, you would also take the administrative exam. If you wish to be more involved with direct patient clinical assisting, you would take the basic and the clinical exam portion.[7] Check your state to see if simply taking the American Association of Medical Assistant's Certified Medical Assistant's exam will qualify you to be a medical assistant with your undergraduate degree.

Early Childhood and Preschool Education

There are many jobs working in childcare and with preschools. Most do not require more than a high school education and therefore do not pay much. However, you should know that jobs working for Head Start programs generally pay more and often provide good benefits. Head Start programs are funded by the federal government in the form of three to five year grants. These grants expect that Head Start program personnel have adequate education and therefore should be paid well. Those graduating with a BA or BS qualify to be an associate teacher if they have taken 12 units of courses related to child development as what is called the Child Development Permit Matrix in California and in many other states.[8] These core courses should be in child or human development. As an associate teacher you perform the duties of a teacher and get paid as one. After starting as a teacher, you will have 10 years to take an additional 15 units of courses to meet the full teacher requirements, if you wish to continue as a teacher beyond 10 years.

Career or Job Counselor

Many social science graduates with a BA choose to work as a career or job training counselor. These positions can be found within a college or at regional vocational or job training centers. Colleges have career centers and often specialty programs for underserved populations that help them succeed in college (e.g., EOP, migrant program, etc.). Outside of colleges, there are regional government and nongovernment programs that offer job finding and training services for those unemployed. Job counselors in such settings provide counseling and support. There are also training and development specialists who often work in human resource departments in private companies, government agencies, or nonprofit organizations that help provide or facilitate specific job training to employees.[9] Human resource (HR) specialists are also bachelor's-level professionals who work in human resource offices. These do sometimes require certificates or licenses, but many start working as HR assistants and work their way up to become specialists or directors of HR departments.

Retail, Food, and Delivery Services

During times of recession, it is sometimes necessary to take jobs in retail, food service, or delivery. Look for jobs that pay you the most and offer benefits. Starbucks and In-N-Out Burger are among those businesses that pay well and provide benefits, including health care insurance. They are also often flexible if you decide to continue your education part-time. Food servers who earn tips can make a decent income. The pandemic crisis and quarantine is causing online companies like Amazon to hire a great number of delivery drivers and warehouse workers and office managers. These companies often pay very well and offer benefits. Keeping busy during a recession and pandemic is important for preventing depression and anxiety. Why not keep busy and earn money at the same time by taking some of these more easily obtainable jobs? When you do work in such "nonprofessional" jobs, make sure to keep track in a notebook the skills, knowledge, training, and experience that you are gaining that will help you land a professional job in the future. Remember, employers who hire college-educated professionals want employees who work well with diverse populations, have excellent interpersonal relationship and communication skills, work well in groups, problem solve, and have excellent critical thinking skills. Often, retail and food service jobs train you and provide you with experience in these areas. As you are working in such jobs, point out to your job supervisor the aforementioned professional skills, training, experience, and knowledge that you are gaining so that they reflect that in a future letter of recommendation or when they are contacted as references.

The purpose of this chapter was to demonstrate the value of your undergraduate degree as it is, with no additional formal training. As you can see, there are many jobs you qualify for with just your BA or BS. Employers value these degrees even if they know that such undergraduate degrees do not necessarily train you for particular jobs, and even if they do (e.g., Bachelor of Social Work), they can also be used for other occupations outside of the field. Your interest and experience is what will allow you to seek jobs in various areas. If for some reason you cannot get into a professional job because of the effects of a recession on the job market, work in any job that you can find and plan on translating your experiences in a nonprofessional job into skills, experiences, knowledge, and training that *is* professional. For example, all professional, well-paying jobs require individuals to have excellent interpersonal relationship and communication skills. You can gain these in many service or retail settings.

Notes

1. U.S. Bureau of Labor Statistics. (2021). *Occupational outlook handbook*. U.S. Department of Labor.

2. Information on CBEST testing can be found at https://www.ctcexams.nesinc.com/PageView.aspx?f=GEN_AboutCBEST.html

3. Information on CSET testing can be found at https://www.ctcexams.nesinc.com/PageView.aspx?f=GEN_AboutCSET.html

4. U.S. Bureau of Labor Statistics. (2021). *Occupational outlook handbook*. U.S. Department of Labor. https://www.bls.gov/ooh/

5. Yate, M. (n.d.). *12 Fastest growing jobs in healthcare: The fastest growing healthcare jobs are also 12 of the 30 fastest growing jobs in all professions*. Monster. https://www.monster.com/career-advice/article/most-stable-professional-sector-healthcare

6. Telemedicine client services associate job posted on the American Telemedicine Association job's website. Accessed on May 20, 2020, at https://americantelemed-jobs.careerwebsite.com/jobs/function/education/

7. California Certifying Board for Medical Assistants. (n.d.). *Certification*. http://www.ccbma.org/exam.html

8. Child Development Training Consortium. (n.d.). *The child development permit matrix*. https://www.childdevelopment.org/cs/cdtc/download/rs/17/Permit%20Matrix%209-07%20SD.pdf?x-r=pcfile_d

9. U.S. Bureau of Labor Statistics. (n.d.). Human resource specialist. In *Occupational outlook handbook*. U.S. Department of Labor. https://www.bls.gov/ooh/business-and-financial/human-resources-specialists.htm

MY OWN NOTES AND REFLECTIONS ON CHAPTER 17

To what extent do you feel your BA or BS degree is sufficient to secure a professional job?

What professional jobs that only require an undergraduate degree would you consider taking? Use the information in the chapter and also in the Occupational Outlook Handbook *mentioned to identify up to three viable careers or occupations you would be interested in pursuing.*

_____

_____

_____

_____

_____

_____

_____

_____

_____

_____

_____

_____

_____

_____

_____

_____

_____

_____

_____

_____

CHAPTER 18

ENHANCE YOUR PROFESSIONAL SKILL SET AND UNDERSTANDING OF HUMAN BEINGS

As mentioned earlier, the American educational system is mostly based on the assumption that a good college education should be a liberal arts education, where students are exposed to a variety of fields, which is what we call general education (e.g., English, social sciences, history, and math). These general education classes add up to about half of the total course units. The other half of your units are classes related to your actual major. The classes for your major are usually courses that give you knowledge of various areas that encompass the field tied to your major. For example, in the major I teach, human development, students take courses that cover the major stages and theories that explain human development across the life span. Usually, students have major electives that they can choose that focus on a particular area within the field (e.g., at-risk youth, gerontology, etc.). The same is true in all majors.

While there may be concentrations within a major that students can choose from, the intent is not to have students become true specialists and prepare them for a particular job or career but rather the education is meant to make the student well-rounded within and outside their chosen major. The U.S. liberal studies concept of education believes in providing students with a lot of knowledge of various fields, allowing them to be resourceful in applying that knowledge to contribute to any task in any particular job or career related or not related to their major. As such, there is an inherent expectation that students will use their interests and passions to continue to build on the knowledge gained from their degree and with time become more specialized once entering a particular field or career. This makes some students who have varied interests anxious because they sometimes have a hard time deciding on a particular career or job. Let me assure you that even for those who know what they want to do, the future will require that they be flexible and open to learning new skill sets.

In a recession, the job or career choices can be significantly reduced due to contractions in the economy, which lead to reduced tax revenues that are used for many health and human service applications. College graduates need to be prepared to fill jobs that might or might not complement their major, degree, or field of interest. That is why you need to work on understanding what you gained from your education and focus on developing or enhancing skills that all employers want to see in their professional employees. These include:

- writing skills
- oral communication skills
- interpersonal relationship skills
- ability to work with diverse populations that include social, economic, developmental, and cultural groups. This includes developing:
  - linguistic abilities (e.g., bi- and multilingualism)
  - cultural sensitivity and competence
- be approachable or likeable, positive, and have a can-do attitude
- work well with others and in groups
- have good critical thinking and problem solving skills
- be able to retrieve, understand, and apply or utilize research or fact-based information
- be adaptable and amenable to change based on needs
- demonstrate extracurricular interests

Most of us are lacking in some of these areas. Go through the list and choose those skills you wish to improve. Make notes on where you feel you stand in relationship to any one of these traits. Make your intent to improve on these traits. Make it fun and an opportunity to develop your social support network by engaging others to monitor your progress. The United States is culturally diverse—most of us are descendants of past or recent immigrants. Hence, we are a multicultural society. Having the ability to work with culturally diverse populations is important and is linked to the ability to work well with others in general. Decide to focus on learning about one particular cultural group—especially if you feel you are likely to work them in professional settings. Learn their dominant cultural values and practices. Learn how various cultures have similarities and differences. For example, an often-cited paper on culture and self explains how world views are different for Asian versus Western cultures. The common Western saying "the squeaky wheel gets the grease" goes counter to the Eastern saying "the nail that stands out gets pounded down."[1] As we learn about specific cultures, we can learn the extent to which different cultures share worldviews or are unique.

However, it is important to also learn about the concepts of acculturation and assimilation to avoid generalizing since many, particularly young, immigrants adopt mainstream culture. Do not make the mistake that some make of complimenting second- or third-generation immigrants on how well they speak English when that was the only language they were taught from birth! Similarly, do not assume that immigrants who are White and Caucasian have assimilated to mainstream culture and think like you do. As always, the solution is to not make assumptions regarding people and to know that we are a country of immigrants that celebrates its cultural roots—past and recent. Commit to learning about the cultures you see and work with. You can do that through reading and researching or by taking a class at your local community college on the language and culture.

Writing well is another very important skill to continually practice and develop. If you are going to be working as a professional, your employer will expect that you are able to communicate well in writing. Always proof your writing, be it emails or documents you produce. Writing is a skill and can thus always be improved with training. Our current focus on sending abbreviated forms of communication through texts or short posts on social media is causing a decline in our ability to complete coherent sentences that convey our thoughts. This leads to ineffective communication, at best, and to misunderstandings, at worst. Karen Hertzberg,[2] a highly skilled writer and editor, reviewed 10 books you can choose from that will help you learn to improve your writing skills. I always find errors when writing an initial draft of an email. That is why proofing your writing and having others review it is so critical.

Colleges with high numbers of first-generation college students commonly have students who struggle with written and oral communication. Problems with oral communication are common because parents and other family members with no college education have a limited vocabulary that they can pass on to their children. While in college we expand our vocabulary, but sometimes it remains limited. Regardless of whether you are an immigrant, focusing on developing your vocabulary can help when presenting yourself as a professional to others. Also, keep in mind that every employment sector has its own vocabulary and lingo. Companies and fields have specialized or favored terms. For example, when I was a doctoral student I heard everyone affiliated with the psychology department use the term epistemology, which was new to me. Every professor seemed to use the term constantly; we seemed to all be deep in epistemological thought. When first hearing it, I am sure I had a deer in front of lights kind of look. So, learn the lingo of the field you wish to go into, beyond increasing your general vocabulary.

Learn a Foreign Language

Use any free time to learn a foreign language. The ideal is to do this while living in a foreign country of native speakers of that language in order to experience immersion. However, you can learn the basics of any language at home on your own. Think about what key things you would need to learn to say if you were in a foreign country where they speak that language. Imagine being there by yourself without anyone to help you. What words or phrases would you consider to be important? Most language courses will begin by teaching such basics as greetings, practical questions like the location of a restroom, and common phrases related to traveling, shopping, and restaurants. If you focus on the very basics, it makes it easier to learn those necessary terms. If you place the basic terms within a career context, will see that other terms or phrases need to be learned as well. For example, if you were a nurse, you would also include phrases such as: Where does it hurt? What is your name and birth date? How long have you had that condition or felt that pain? Give me or raise your hand, arm, or leg. Take a deep breath.

Always imagine being in a specific setting and working with clients who speak the language you wish to learn; that will guide you on the basics in the language. Once you have the basic terms identified, practice the pronunciation because that is what gets people in trouble, including myself when I speak Spanish with my in-laws from Mexico. You will experience particular challenges with certain sounds common in some languages that are not shared in the English language. For example, we do not roll our *r*'s in English as they do in Spanish or in German. Pronunciation takes practice and a lot of close listening to the sound of the language being spoken.

Another good way to learn a foreign language is to watch movies with English subtitles while paying attention to the sound of the language so you can get used to the sounds of it, the sound of specific words and phrases. Once you have achieved even a rudimentary level of knowledge and pronunciation of basic words and phrases, you can put down on your resume that you have a basic understanding and ability to communicate in that language. If you do not know which language to learn, I would say choose Spanish because of the large size of the Spanish speaking population in the United States. Another good one to consider is American Sign Language.

Knowledge of Developmental Stages

This might be a bias, since I am in a professor of human development, but having paid close attention to development, I can see that understanding people within the context of their age is very important for relating to and understanding people. This can help you to be more patient with age-stage groups on both ends of the continuum—the very young and the very old. Some of you may have taken a course that at least briefly covered age stages. Certainly, human development students took classes that taught them about every single stage of human life, from birth to death. I encourage these and others to find an introductory textbook and to review the main developmental characteristics of each major developmental age group or stage in life. Pay particular attention to the one that you are likely to work with in your current or future professional job or career. This is something that few people think about in specific terms. It is important not to make overgeneralizations regarding age stages, such as referring to someone as an old man. An old man for one person may mean a 40-year-old, whereas it could mean a 90-year-old for another. Once you learn about human development, you have the capacity to not only educate others around you about how developmental stages differ but also how they overlap and even differ from person to person. Pay particular attention to your own age stage and its developmental mandates since they will also let you know why you might have certain emotions, attitudes, needs, and behavioral tendencies.

According to research, a developmental mandate for young adults is dealing with intimacy and isolation.[3] That is, young adults between the ages of 19 and about 40 focus on developing relationships, including intimate relationships, such as with a spouse or significant other. Knowing this trait of young adults allows you to learn what your own needs are and why forming relationships seem so important to you. To be sensitive to various developmental stages, you need to start with learning about your own stage. That will allow you to better appreciate and relate to other stages in life. This principle of knowing yourself first is important and is reflected in training programs for developing cultural sensitivity and competence, such as that by Paul Pedersen.[4] Learning about human development will help you understand and relate well with others.

Learn About the Complex Interplay of "BioPsychoSocioGenDevEcoPoliHisto" and Cultural Factors

I remember as a doctoral student in psychology, I was introduced to the psycho-social and cultural understanding of thought and behavior. By the time I finished my doctorate, the term and associated theoretical models expanded to favoring a biopsychosocial cultural framework. Over the last few years, I have noticed that human behavior and thought is influenced by a variety of additional factors that include our biology, genetics, psychology or mental health, sociology or social group, gender, developmental stage, socioeconomic status, and political factors, including how politics assigns us value based on our culture or physical characteristics.

History also plays a critical, yet overlooked, role. History includes how communities continue to react to or appreciate one group over others. You can imagine the importance of the interplay of all these factors that determine our mental state, behavior, health, and sense of worth. This complex interplay of factors is not yet well understood, but there is increased awareness of their importance. For example, even companies are starting to engage multidisciplinary teams to tackle problems from the development of new products to their marketing strategy.

This is the current world that we are in. Do not be afraid of complexity; welcome it. Consider the complexity of understanding others as you work with diverse populations and use that knowledge of our complexity to avoid stereotyping cultural groups, understanding that behavior or attitudes may not be as much due to culture but to other factors, such as income and education. After all, we have recognized for some time the existence of the culture of poverty.[5] As the anthropologist Oscar Lewis suggested, a subculture develops out of generations of poverty that mold or shape "the worldview, aspirations, and character of the children who grow up in it," which then get passed on generationally.[6] Do not confuse traditional cultural characteristics with behaviors, attitudes, and emotions that are more reflective of a culture of poverty or long-term experience with scarcity of resources. Become complex in your thinking because that is more in keeping with reality than what we tend to assume.

If you find yourself unemployed or underemployed in nonprofessional jobs, you should not lose hope in finding a career that uses your college degree. As you wait for the job market to improve, plan on developing the skills discussed in this chapter. Simply wishing to improve your professional skills is not enough. You need to make a plan. Decide on those skills you need to work on the most, such as writing or verbal communication. Earlier chapters also gave you advice on ways to improve some of these skills. One of the most important messages of this chapter is that the people you will be working with in whatever field you are in are likely to be diverse and complex. This diversity is likely to be based on factors such as culture, developmental stages, or educational and socioeconomic status, among others, including working with or serving persons having unique historical past experiences (e.g., origins in another country, serving as a military member in Iraq, etc.). Consider those diversity factors that are most relevant given the people you will be working with as colleagues, clients, or patients. This will make you uniquely prepared to compete for professional jobs.

Notes

1. Cherry, K. (2019). *Intimacy vs. isolation: Psychosocial stage 6.* Very Well Mind. https://www.verywellmind.com/intimacy-versus-isolation-2795739

2. Hertzberg, K. (2019). 10 amazing books that will improve your writing skills. *Grammarly.* https://www.grammarly.com/blog/books-that-improve-writing-skills/

3. Cherry, K. (2019). *Intimacy vs. isolation: psychosocial stage 6.* Very Well Mind. https://www.verywellmind.com/intimacy-versus-isolation-2795739

4. Pedersen, P. (1988). *Handbook for developing multicultural awareness.* American Association for Counseling and Development.

5. Culture of poverty. (2020). In *Wikipedia.* https://en.wikipedia.org/wiki/Culture_of_poverty

6. Lewis, O. (1969). Culture of poverty. In D. P. Moynihan (Ed.), *Understanding poverty: Perspectives from the social sciences.* Basic Books, p. 199.

MY OWN NOTES AND REFLECTIONS ON CHAPTER 18

What did you think about this chapter's suggestion for you to increase your professional skill set? Come up with a list of skills you wish to develop or improve that will make you more competitive professionally. Develop a specific method and timeline for developing the skills you have outlined.

What is your knowledge and training in understanding the complex diversity of those you work with or serve or wish to serve in the future? Identify those skills you think would enhance your professional preparation, including the possibility of learning a new language. Read about the age stages of those you are likely to work with, including your own, and write out the dominant characteristics of each stage in terms of their normative cognition, emotions, and attitudes.

CHAPTER 19

ACKNOWLEDGE AND BUILD YOUR PROFESSIONAL NETWORK

I n a career preparation class I teach, I often have speakers come who share their experiences of getting to their current position, which typically is a very successful position, be it as nurse, doctor, social worker, scientist, researcher, or public health worker, to name a few. They consistently mention the importance of people they met who influenced them and helped them get to their current position. Who you know is critical for your advancement professionally, and that is why the topic of networking deserves its own chapter. An earlier chapter covered the importance of social support and social networks. This chapter covers professional networks and networking. This type of social networking is specialized and focused on the professional realm. Your *professional network* is composed of those who can help you succeed and advance professionally. *Networking* is the behavioral action of reaching out to professionals to either add them to your professional network or to seek their assistance in finding or securing a professional position or advancement. Your professional network and networking are particularly important during a recession because it is during this time that you will experience the greatest competition for fewer jobs, seats, or admission within graduate programs.

Know That Those Deciding Your Fate Are Human

Let us start by discussing this important topic with mentioning a basic fact: We are all human beings—both bosses and employees. This is a fact you need to remember. I know that it sounds strange to say what seems obvious, but the fact is that we often fail to acknowledge that bosses and decision makers are human beings when it comes to us applying for jobs or needing information or assistance. We fail to realize that the applications we send out are acted on by human beings—even when computer scanners are used to screen or weed out some applications not meeting basic criteria, which is sometimes done by large employers. In the end, even in large organizations, human beings have to decide the fate of each applicant. Human beings are also those who ask you questions, listen to your responses, and note your answers to questions during job interviews. Human beings will deliberate on whether to make you a job offer or accept you into a graduate program. Being that we are talking about human beings, we also have to understand that, as human beings, we are persuaded by personal biases. Sometimes these biases favor us and at other times they do not.

Power of Being Known and Knowing Others

Even with biases, what I can assure you of is this: Being known by a confidant or friend of the employer or graduate program almost always leads to significant advantages. That is why many of my students who volunteer at organizations for their field experience end up being hired by the organization in which they volunteered. Again, networking is the number one suggestion that classroom speakers consistently give to students when discussing what they can do to improve their chances of getting a job or of succeeding in a career.

How Your Professional Network Benefits You

People in your network benefit you in at least three ways. First, they validate you and serve to recommend you. Second, people in your network can serve as psychological support and can encourage you to pursue your goals, boosting your self-confidence. Third, people in your network are also sources of important information. For example, they can inform you of opportunities you did not know about. They can also know when you should or should not apply. I remember considering applying for a job as an administrator. A person in my network who was an insider suggested, in their words, "Don't waste your time. They know who they want to hire already." At other times, the opposite happens: "You really should apply. They told me they liked you and that they decided they would consider people like you even if you do not meet all the minimal qualifications!"

Put Effort into Building Your Professional Network

I might have convinced you to pay attention to your professional network, but you may say, "But my network is little or puny!" Clearly, as a new college graduate, you need to build your professional network. There are two things you can do to build your network. First, acknowledge and document your existing network. You probably already know a lot of people who can help you in the ways outlined above. The problem is that you probably never took stock of them or considered them as part of your professional network. So, the first step is to use your career notebook, which I suggest you have, to list all relatives and nonrelatives who you think can: (1) validate you and serve as a character reference or recommender, (2) be of psychological support to you or be your cheerleader when applying or looking for job opportunities, and (3) provide you with valuable information about opportunities you may not be aware of or give you honest feedback on possible jobs or graduate programs. Besides relatives and friends of the family, think of past counselors, teachers, neighbors, school and work peers—anyone you have had any relationship with. Next to the name of each person you list as a potential source of support, indicate the extent to which they are indeed an enthusiastic supporter of yours. You may know someone and you can say how they can be helpful, but you need to also note how enthusiastic they would be as supporters of yours at this present time. Therefore, do not simply write out a list of people in your professional network but also note what role they can possibly play for you, along with their likely level of enthusiasm. Sometimes people on your network list can serve all three functions. If so, note that.

The second thing to do after developing your professional network list is to note or highlight those who can most help you with your current priorities, to serve as a recommender or to bounce off ideas—whatever your current need is. Plan on contacting them to establish or reestablish a relationship with them. For example, if you know of a professor who you took a past class from and is relevant to your need, but you really did not develop rapport with them and it has been a while since communicating with them, consider starting to do so by sending them an email informing them of what you are now doing and what you plan on doing in the future in terms of securing a job or entry into a graduate program. Relationships take time to make and maintain. That time needs to translate into communication and contact. Of course, there is nothing like in-person contact with people when building a relationship and for gaining their support. However, physical distance or the current pandemic crisis can make in-person contact impractical, so using technological mediums, such as video conferencing, phone calls, or emails, will have to do for now. If possible, use a medium like Zoom or some visual communication method since it is second best from in-person contact.

Searching for New Supporters

After you have compiled a list of people you already know for your professional network, you should search for those you do not know who can serve as supporters, sources of information, or outright employers. For example, I may want to get a job in a particular organization because I can see myself working there, perhaps because they also pay well, but I do not have anyone in my network who works there to help me. Consider going through the organization's website to learn about it and to find personnel who can help you to learn more about the organization and about opportunities for employment. Consider asking to do an informational interview to learn more about their experience as a professional working in the organization. Make sure to give them a reason why they were chosen by you. A good reason may be that you found specific things that you share in common with them based on their online biography. Make sure to point out those things that you admire about them that inspired you to contact them. If you provide a good justification for contacting them, you will see that most people will be excited to meet you or to talk to you by phone if you reflect knowledge and appreciation of them. After securing their support, you can then add them to your professional networking list.

Attend Talks, Events, and Other Presentations

Attending presentations, lectures, and events, like career fairs and workshops, is a great way to boost your career network. Many are happening remotely through Zoom, which may make it even easier to meet and start dialogue with representatives of organizations of interest. After the pandemic crisis, do not stay home moping. Attend various functions and talks where you know that people are likely to be who can inform you of opportunities or simply be of psychological, emotional, or practical support to you. When you attend events and presentations, become a social butterfly and make a point of introducing yourself to people. Acknowledge and learn their names. Note them in your notebook to remember them. Follow up with email greetings and notes of appreciation. I guarantee you that if you do what I am suggesting, you will significantly add to your professional networking list and you will learn of new opportunities.

Use LinkedIn

LinkedIn is fast becoming an important way of finding jobs and of adding to your career network. LinkedIn is an online platform that allows you to develop your professional profile that viewers like employers can use to find you and even offer you a job. It has a free version and a premium account that costs about $25 per month without a contract. The premium account provides *InMail*, which allows you to receive email messages, see more profiles of individuals you search for, provides greater number of search filters, and offers more targeted searches, in addition to a few other features. However, the free account is fine for most applications. With a free account you can still contact people by inviting them to be added to your network. Decide on what you will emphasize in your LinkedIn profile so that it conveys something specific that you want to emphasize about yourself, such as the job or career you are pursuing. The more focused you are in your professional interests, the more likely you are to have employers and other people contacting you.

The most important function of LinkedIn for graduating college students is in helping you find people to add to your network who can assist you in identifying and securing a job or entry into a graduate program. You can search, for example, for alumni from your university who are currently employed in the professional roles you are interested in (e.g., computer scientists, lab technicians, teachers, nurses or social workers, speech and language pathologist, etc.). People are always happy to make contact with those who have just graduated from the same school and program and who can benefit from their expertise, experience, and knowledge. If you can, attend some of your university's career center presentations or workshops that offer training on using LinkedIn to help you learn how to best build your most visible, appealing, and professional profile and how to best network using LinkedIn. LindedIn has actual job listings for you to look at as well. LinkedIn has been rated third place, by some,[1] in being a good online job search engine.

Join Your University's Alumni Association

I recommend joining your university's alumni association, making sure you also join the chapter tied to your specific major. This is a great way for you to become familiar with others who graduated from the same school and program but are working in various fields that may be of interest to you. Alumni chapters hold events throughout the year, which are fun and are excellent ways of learning from your older peers. Also consider getting involved as an officer with your school's alumni association or with a chapter. That way you have even more opportunities for interacting with alumni. If you join, make sure to network with your peers; many join alumni associations and only put their affiliation on their resume, failing to use their membership for actual networking.

Another benefit of joining the alumni association right after graduation is that some schools allow you continued access to programs and services on campus. For example, if you are an alum at Cal State San Marcos, you get to keep your university email and get continued access to the library and career center services for as long as you are an alum. Just having access to the career center is worth every cent paid for alumni membership. The career center has career counselors who can sit down with you and give personal feedback and advice on job searches, applications, resumes, cover letters, and career choices in general. They also give you access to online programs, such as Big Interview, which help you prepare for interviews by giving you advice and examples of good interviews. That feature alone saves you the $79 dollars a month you would pay for it online. Career centers commonly offer access to many career tests, such as career interest, aptitude, or personality inventory tests, that help you learn more about yourself. Finally, as an alum, perhaps you may be able to attend specialty workshops and job fairs. At least for our university, it is a bargain paying for alumni membership when you get so many services. If you join your alumni association and chapter, please do make sure to be appraised of the benefits of being a member and take advantage of all of them.

Informational Interviews

An informational interview is when you interview someone who is in a career that is directly of interest to you. You may be considering getting a graduate degree in computer science because you are interested in programming. Consider interviewing someone who works as a programmer and who holds a master's degree to find out what it is like working as a programmer. They can give you advice on graduate programs and classes to pay particular attention to, as well as what employers are the best in the field. Alternatively, you can conduct an informational interview with someone who is in a job that you now qualify for with your degree, such as a case manager. They can not only tell you what it is like but also might be able to help you get a job in their organization.

Being a recent graduate, professionals will see you as someone possessing the latest in knowledge regarding the field that you represent. They will be most eager to help you launch your career. I estimate that the window of excitement about you being a recent graduate is about one to three years after graduation. Of course, it all depends on how you introduce yourself. For example, three years after graduation, you could say to someone you wish to interview, "Hi, I'm a relatively recent college graduate interested in learning about your occupation" and that would be accurate since three years is relatively recent as far as graduating from college is concerned. The point is that you should make sure that you make yourself worth devoting time to. Being contacted or meeting a recent graduate is always exciting for most professionals representing organizations and professions that you are interested in.

This chapter emphasizes the importance of developing and nurturing professional relationships so as to have you develop and maintain your professional network. Most successful professionals will tell you that their success was a result of support they received from people who believed in them and decided to help and encourage them. Building your professional network is critical to your success in the professional world. Professional networks are particularly important during serious economic recessions since jobs and graduate program seats become scarce and very competitive. Employers and graduate programs representatives are all humans who respond to social interactions with other humans. Being known is critical to your success. Writing great applications is important, but turning them into those who recognize you is what will land you employment offers.

Note

1. Career Sidekick. (2020). *The top 10 job search engines for 2020.* https://careersidekick.com/tools/job-search-websites/

MY OWN NOTES AND REFLECTIONS ON CHAPTER 19

Questions and activities to consider, besides your own notes.

Describe your current professional network. Who is in your professional network, and what purpose do they serve for you? If you do not have one, develop one and start by listing the type of people who will help you. That will guide you in searching for those to put into your network.

Come up with plans for either creating or enhancing your LinkedIn profile. Using LinkedIn, conduct a search of graduates from your college or university who have the same degree as you and find out what they are doing. Start a conversation with those on that list who are in jobs or occupations that are of interest to you, asking them about their experiences in those jobs or occupations.

What advantages do you derive from becoming a member of your university's alumni association? Is there an alumni chapter tied to your specific degree or major that you can get involved with? Use the information in the chapter to come up with plans to increase your professional network.

_____

_____

_____

_____

_____

_____

_____

_____

_____

_____

_____

_____

_____

_____

PART IV

PERSONAL CONSIDERATIONS

CHAPTER 20

HANDLING STRESS, ANXIETY, AND DEPRESSION

Three common outcomes from unemployment and financial hardship are high levels of stress, anxiety, and depression. I remember when I was toward the end of my graduate program for my doctorate and I was applying for my first permanent job. I still had to finish writing my dissertation and defend it. I moved my family from Boulder, Colorado, to San Diego, California, to take a paid internship with the U.S. Navy. After the internship, I did not want to go back to Boulder; I decided to stay in San Diego while finishing my dissertation and continue to work for the Navy. While working on my dissertation, at the end of my paid internship, there was a wait period of about two months until my application for a federal job as a researcher was finished being processed. I was verbally assured by the navy research center that I would likely secure the research job, but the wait of two months was totally stressful because I had no income to support my wife and young children. I felt stressed, anxious, and, for the first time, depressed and had a low sense of self-worth. I tried looking for other positions, even retail jobs, to keep my finances going to no avail. I had two small children and a wife to take care of and I felt like a failure to them.

All of those negative feelings came as soon as I stopped earning income as an intern researcher. I found out that you do not have to be considered a weak person or somehow deficient to experience a downward sense of self-concept and experience a flood of negative emotions. If you are going through what I went through, just know that your emotions are valid, but they are also temporary. You need to know that you are not the only one who has these self-doubts and negative emotions. Your feelings and emotions are normal given the circumstances. There are things you can do to reduce your negative emotions. You may not be able to eliminate them, but a reduction is realistic and possible. This chapter will give you options for seeking help.

Talk to Others and Get Informed

The first thing to do when you are feeling down because of your employment situation is to talk with others who are also going through the same experience and feel the same way. Luckily, we now have email, social media, and nationwide free calls that allow you to communicate with people who care for you and can listen to you. Doing so will give you a sense of validation of your emotions and make you not feel alone. The second thing you should do is reach out to those who can help you feel better and who may have practical advice for you. These include those who have gone through the same experience in the past, such as university alumni who graduated with the same major, and also those who can simply empathize or at least sympathize with you, such as career counselors. Such sympathy and empathy can validate your feelings and, in turn, you.

Get information from the people you talk to about emerging opportunities for either employment or training, including internships. Read the newspaper, especially the business section, to see what the local hiring trends are and what employment training programs are emerging. Social media platforms, such as Facebook, Instagram, and Twitter, are a great alternative to the newspaper because through them you can join many like-minded groups that keep you informed. Use them to stay abreast of economic developments. Use those you know, as well as your graduating peers, to keep you apprised of opportunities for jobs or training. This type of information will help reduce your stress and anxiety by giving you leads on job or career opportunities.

You may follow the aforementioned advice and still feel depressed and down. If so, it is important to know the distinction between feeling depressed or down but still being able to act and being incapacitated psychologically, feeling frozen and unable to act or feel any optimism or hope. If you feel like the latter, then take advantage of professional help, such as help from a therapist or psychological counselor. It is like when a car is stuck in mud and sand and the wheels just spin without the car moving. If you are frozen, you should get help from a professional. It does not mean that you are mentally ill or need major psychiatric intervention. It is just that you, like all of us, sometimes need that jump start that comes from seeing a professional counselor or therapist. You may be able to secure such professional help from the university you graduated from, such as from the student health center. If you are covered by a health insurance plan, see if they cover visits with a therapist. Most counties, parishes, or boroughs have mental health divisions and they can also help you if you cannot afford a therapist or need a referral.

For example, in San Diego County, there are community agencies that can help because they either have therapeutic services available or they can refer you out to those that can help you. Below is a list of helpful organizations in the San

Diego region that will give you a sense of the types of organizations that you can find in your particular state and county. Even if you are in a different state, look at these organizations and become familiar with the type of services and programs they have. It will give you an example of organizations you can search for in your state and region. Many of these organizations offer mental health or behavioral health services.

- **Lifeline Coastal Community Services in Oceanside**
  - URL: https://www.nclifeline.org/
- **Interfaith Community Services in Escondido**
  - URL: http://www.interfaithservices.org/
- **Center for Community Solutions in Escondido**
  - URL: https://www.ccssd.org/
- **North County Health Services in San Marcos, Encinitas, and Oceanside**
  - URL: https://www.nchs-health.org/
- **Vista Community Clinic in Vista**
  - URL: http://www.vistacommunityclinic.org/locations/
- **Community Resource Center in Encinitas**
  - URL: https://crcncc.org/
- **Community Interface Services**
  - URL: http://www.communityinterfaceservices.org/
- **Women's Resource Center in Oceanside**
  - URL: https://www.wrcsd.org/

Develop a list of comparable mental health service agencies in your area. The easiest thing to do when developing a list of helpful agencies is to talk to any local or regional community service agency that offers case management or social work type of services. They will be able to help you develop your list of agencies to contact for help. You can also call any of the many national hotlines that are set up to help you find services in your particular area. The Victim Connect Resource Center website has a list of most national hotlines.[1] You can also call the toll-free number (855-4-Victim). Believe me, once you take that important first step of admitting you need help, you will be glad you sought it! When it comes to mental health, it is always best to seek help from people, especially professionals, and not to try to solve things on our own. Once you hear the voice of help, you will be glad for it and your stress level will go down immediately.

This chapter starts the last section of the book on personal considerations, such as stress, anxiety, and depression. It is common to experience all three of these during serious recessions. That is normal and we need to know that there is light at the end of the dark tunnel. However, during the wait, we need to recognize that we sometimes need help to get out of our stressed, anxious, and depressed state that often immobilizes us. Being surrounded by others who support us and can serve as sounding boards is critical. Sometimes things seem too overwhelming to the point that we become immobilized, unable to act in any way to help ourselves get out of our current situation. Examples of the type of organizations available in your state and county are provided as well as national hotlines that can give you good referral sources. The important thing is to not let yourself stay immobile or frozen. Get help from professionals who can unfreeze you and give you a sense of hope and even optimism.

Note

1. Victim Connect Resource Center. (n.d.). *National Hotlines*. https://victimconnect. org/resources/national-hotlines/

MY OWN NOTES AND REFLECTIONS ON CHAPTER 20

Questions and activities to consider, besides your own notes.

What are the different problems or situations causing you stress right now? Which were pre-existing and which are new or postpandemic or economic crisis? What are your symptoms of stress (e.g., anxiety, feeling stressed, unable to sleep, crying, etc.)? What are some effective strategies you know of that you can use to minimize your stress (e.g., mindfulness, meditation), and how helpful have they been?

Who do you have to talk to about your concerns and stress? If you lack people to talk to, develop strategies for finding people who you can trust to talk to.

Develop a list of mental health agencies in your area, including government offices (e.g., county health, social, or behavioral health services offices) that you can contact for help if you feel stressed, anxious, and depressed. Identify at least one helping agency you are inclined to call to get help for your particular feeling and situation.

CHAPTER 21

INFLUENCE OF SUBSTANCES AND MEDICATIONS

Society has taught us to take substances to alleviate stress, anxiety, or depression. How often do you see movies where a stressed or upset protagonist says "I need a drink"? Such characters will be shown going to a bar to have a strong drink or many drinks, and yet, amazingly, they do not get drunk and are able to hold a conversation. Alternatively, they will be shown acting silly or funny, getting tipsy if not drunk. Somehow, they do not look out of control. Pharmaceutical companies also lobby doctors and health professionals, promising their patients help for when they are stressed or anxious. Psychotropic drugs, like antidepressants, have their place, but we also know that they are often prescribed too loosely and too often by medical doctors. The current opioid crisis demonstrates the challenges we face when we rely too much on substances to help us get us through painful and stressful times.

Unless you have a diagnosed mental illness, my suggestion to you is to not take any substances to help you with your stress, anxiety, or depression—legal or otherwise. I say this for several reasons. First, it will only help you temporarily. Second, and most important, by taking drugs or substances we are developing a pattern of dependency where we automatically seek substances, like alcohol, to alter our mood and regulate our emotions. There are other things that can better help you cope with the stress, anxiety, and depression. Exercise and social interaction are examples of healthy activities you can do that have more lasting positive outcomes for you and that alter your emotions and future outlook. One thing to know is that most psychotropic drugs, like antidepressants, alter your mind in sometimes permanent or long term ways and can cause you to become aggressive and/or suicidal—something that you were not before. I have a nephew that is in that situation and now he cannot see himself ever being free of his psychotropic drugs because they are so deeply imbedded in his daily life. Fight the societal trend and stay mentally and physically healthy!

Alcohol

The other drug to keep away from during stressful times is alcohol. It can lead to dependency and, being a depressant, can negatively affect our mood and future outlook. Studies show that it also affects levels of anxiety and stress the day after drinking even if drinking was done in moderation. That can lead to fights with those around us, including the very loved ones we depend on for support during a serious recession. Drinking also affects cognition, inhibiting our memory recall, which we need when problem solving. Resist the temptation to drink and see for yourself the difference in your mental aptitude and mood compared to when you drink. You will see that your mind is clearer and your emotions are more stable. You will also react to others very differently and more positively if you do not drink. You will notice that you sleep better when not drinking. Alcohol can cause us to feel sleepy when under the influence, but in reality, it causes our sleep to be disrupted. Drinking almost always negatively affects those who are around us, those we depend on for our emotional support.

This short chapter is important in pointing out a common problem we all have when we are stressed and anxious about our career or economic situation. Society, unfortunately, promotes the concept of taking substances or medications when we are not feeling happy or when we are stressed and anxious. We need to not fall victim to the pressure to drink or take substances to alter our mood. There are other activities that have a much more positive impact on our mood and feelings that are more long lasting, such as exercise and being surrounded by people who care about us and are not addicted to substances. If you have a problem with substances and mental health, you can call the national substance abuse hotline operated by the Substance Abuse and Mental Health Services Administration Department (SAMHSA), which is available 24/7: 1-800-662-4357. They have trained counselors who can help you during a crisis and can refer you out to more local services available to you.

MY OWN NOTES AND REFLECTIONS
ON CHAPTER 21

Questions and activities to consider, besides your own notes.

What substances or medications do you feel you use to calm yourself or to lower your stress? Describe the challenges you have with these substances (e.g., hangover, dependence on them, anxiety, etc.). If you honestly answer these questions, you will likely find negative consequences from taking substances. Focus on these and develop a plan for reducing and ultimately eliminating them from your use. Seek out a professional to help you with that.

Identify replacement activities that you can do instead use of substances, including alcohol, such as exercising, getting together with friends who do not rely on substances, joining support groups, developing hobbies that get you involved with others, and so on.

_____

_____

_____

_____

_____

_____

_____

_____

_____

_____

_____

_____

_____

_____

_____

_____

_____

CHAPTER 22

IMPORTANCE OF MAINTAINING A DAILY SCHEDULE

P eople who retire after many years commonly find that they are at risk of developing depression immediately after retiring because they go from having a life full of structure and activities to one that has no structure and few required activities. The recession and pandemic crisis is showing students the importance of having structure in their lives. I have heard from students who are having a hard time staying at home, which is precisely what they have to do to avoid being infected during a pandemic. Their anxiety, stress, and depression commonly make them immobile and unable to help themselves or to see the light at the end of the tunnel. The lack of structure in their lives makes them more fearful of the future since they have little else to do than to think and worry, void of keeping to a schedule or routine.

Luckily, many students have learned to successfully cope by building structure in their daily lives. They set a schedule of when to get up, eat, do their homework, contact friends, visit their social media pages, and watch TV or listen to music. That structure helps them to feel more secure and to see that life can be predictable, which leads to having faith and hope. Right now, the U.S. economy is fluctuating and reacting to the pandemic, but when the pandemic is over and the economy recovers, if you find yourself still unemployed, developing structure in your life will help lessen the anxiety and stress you would otherwise have.

Develop a schedule for sleeping, eating, communicating, reading, and exercising. It is also a good for you to limit your TV or online screen time, being mindful of how much time you spend on social media, watching shows and movies, or playing video games. These forms of entertainment are undeniable blessings to those stuck at home, but it is a good idea to consume them in moderation and remember to spend some time outside every day. Include in your schedule reading about how people got through similar crises. Schedule talking to others who are going through your own particular experience and get advice from them on developing structure in your daily life, but reciprocate by giving them advice as well. Make sure you adhere to the schedule that you come up with. Even if you find that some parts of your planned schedule are not realistic, have enough structure in your life so that you feel that sense of security that comes from knowing what to do throughout the day.

When you get up, shower and get dressed as you did before any crisis or recession like when you had to go to work or school. Showering in the morning tells your mind that you are starting anew, getting ready for what the day brings. Dressing professionally is a trick for telling your mind that you are indeed a professional who is prepared to welcome the world as a professional compared to staying in pajamas, which serves as a reminder to your brain that something is wrong and not normal. Pajamas simply tell your mind and body to expect sleeping, slouching, and engaging in nonprofessional activities. Dressing professionally also affects how others react to you as a professional, conveying respect and optimism. Imagine how you would feel if you went to visit a friend in the middle of the day and you found them in their pajamas or in shorts and a t-shirt when you expected to maybe go out with them to apply for professional jobs. You would probably react to them very differently than if you found them in casual, but professional clothes. This mirrors the way that we react to our own dress.

One of the simple messages of this chapter is that structure is critical for us to not feel down and is important for staying positive and for improving our optimism regarding our professional employment status. Our dress is also critical for helping us to feel and act like a professional. Please remember that daily structure helps us have hope and dressing professionally reminds us and others that we are professionals even if we currently do not have a job or are underemployed. Contacting friends who share the same career goals will also help.

MY OWN NOTES AND REFLECTIONS
ON CHAPTER 22

Describe your daily life and schedule before and after the pandemic and economic crisis. What has changed, and how has it affected your mood and level of activity tied to securing a job or entry into a graduate program?

What were your past waking and sleeping time patterns, and what are they now? Develop a realistic schedule for yourself that includes bathing and getting dressed professionally in the morning. Identify specific, engaging, and necessary activities that help you secure a job or entry into a graduate program that you need to do daily over the next seven days.

If you are having a hard time developing and adhering to a daily schedule, talk with confidants or friends. Jointly support one another to develop and keep to a structured schedule. Once you have that, focus on the benefits that you feel coming from adhering to a structured schedule, including an increased sense of security.

_____

_____

_____

_____

_____

_____

_____

_____

_____

_____

_____

_____

_____

_____

_____

_____

CHAPTER 23

IMPORTANCE OF YOUR BODY IN INFLUENCING YOUR MOOD

The Importance of Sleep

Early during the pandemic, I remember not sleeping well or well enough on a particular day. I tried to be positive, but I found that I became overly critical of others, including my wife and mother-in-law who is staying with us because she suffers from an immunity disease and my wife wants to be able to care for her during this pandemic crisis. I knew well that morning that I had not slept enough and I told myself to be careful and not get into trouble by being mean, biting, or critical toward those around me. I told myself to try to act "normal." It was so hard to hide my jitteriness and inclination to say critical things to reveal my lack of sleep and anxious state. As much as I tried, I found I could not do it. I ended up criticizing my wife and warned my mother-in-law to not order my wife around like she was a little girl (something she really does not do). I hardly ever react that way and I usually control my emotions and what I say. However, my body and mind were sleep deprived and there were physical and mental consequences to that, which led to negative outcomes and the establishment of a tense atmosphere in my home that day. I later took a nap and that helped tremendously. It helped so much that I ended up reacting to my wife and mother-in-law positively and amicably.

Sleep deprivation will do that to me and it will do that to you as well. Make sure you get enough sleep, but do not overdo it either since too much sleep will also have the same negative effect on your mood. Plan on at least seven, if not eight, hours of sleep. I did not mention sleep in the earlier chapter on the importance of developing structure in your life, but establishing a stable sleeping pattern with set times to sleep and wake will enhance your mood, emotions, optimism and outlook towards life, yourself, and towards others around you.

Physical Activity and Nutrition

There are two other things that affect your body that you need to pay attention to: physical activity and nutrition. The pandemic has forced us to stay in our homes, where we find ourselves facing the same walls around us 24/7. We all need to be physically active in order to maintain a healthy body and mind. Exercise causes neurotransmitters, such as endorphins, to be produced, which affect our mood positively. Serotonin, for example, which increases with exercise, is associated with a sense of well-being and happiness.

Develop a schedule of exercise that includes at least 20 minutes of cardio a day, keeping your heart rate up for at least 20 minutes. It does not need to be strenuous exercise. Taking brisk walks for 20 minutes every day will do the trick. Use that time to think and plan. Go with a buddy, your spouse, or significant other and use that time to communicate your thoughts and career plans. What you will find is that your mood will improve, stress and anxiety will lessen, and your thinking will be more sharp and creative. Exercising during economic hard times is critical and its benefits to you cannot be over emphasized.

Nutrition

Nutrition is the other part of keeping your body healthy and prepared to handle stress and anxiety. Unfortunately, we are taught or influenced by advertisers to eat snacks like potato chips, cookies, and worst of all, sugary soda drinks. All highly processed foods containing high amounts of starches and sugars alter our mood. Carbs, sweets, and processed food initially spike or elevate our mood for a few minutes, only to have an abrupt drop, making us feel sleepy, groggy, irritable, anxious, and pessimistic. Instead of starchy and sweet processed foods and drink, eat natural foods and vegetables that moderate your sugar levels and therefore your mood. Watch what you eat and drink and see how your diet and nutrition determine how you feel physically and mentally.

This book serving as a survival manual for handling a recession is not complete without discussing the importance of physical activity and nutrition. Taking care of your body is important for maintaining a positive outlook toward life and for handling the stress that comes from living through a major recession and pandemic crisis. Develop a structure in your life that incorporates sleeping well, getting exercise, and eating/drinking wisely. The combination of these three factors will contribute significantly to you achieving your career goal and to you finding solutions to your financial challenges.

MY OWN NOTES AND REFLECTIONS ON CHAPTER 23

Questions and activities to consider, besides your own notes.

How well do you sleep? What barriers do you have for developing a structured sleeping pattern?

How healthy do you feel? Describe your exercise and meal pattern previous to the current pandemic or economic downturn. Point out what has changed and identify the areas of concern. Develop a plan of action for how you can realistically incorporate a schedule of exercise and nutritional meal plan into your daily life for at least the next seven days. Afterwards, maintain or alter the plan to reap its health benefits.

_____

_____

_____

_____

_____

_____

_____

_____

_____

_____

_____

_____

_____

_____

_____

_____

_____

_____

_____

_____

CHAPTER 24

ENGAGING IN CONFLICT WITH INTIMATE PARTNERS, FAMILY, AND FRIENDS

You have probably noticed that when you are stressed or anxious you tend to be moody and reactive with those around you. The fact of the matter is that few families know how to handle stress and anxiety. Many of us have not had good role models in our parents to teach us how to communicate and relate to one another, particularly when stressed. As a result, when stressed and anxious, the average family tends to argue, each member automatically defending each other, being quick to blame others for everything. I am a psychologist who has studied communication, yet my wife and I still find it difficult to communicate sometimes, even when we are not stressed, let alone when we are. We tend to guess at motives and assume that each is thinking how to "win" an argument.

Communication

Even if there is no stress and mistrust, communication can be challenging. One reason is that each person has their own point of reference or perspective that is often different from that of others. For example, if someone says, "Boy, life is not fair," one person hearing it may be thinking about their employer and may assume that what the person means is that employers are not fair because they do not pay employees what they are worth. Yet, for someone else hearing that same statement who was recently thinking about lower than expected grades received on assignments in school, they might be thinking about the unfairness of universities or professors or the particular assignments. The point is that miscommunication is tied to different frames of reference that often lead to misunderstandings and mistrust, which can then lead to conflict and fighting.

We need to know that we have control over what we say and how we react toward others, which will determine whether an escalation of tension is occurring or whether the opposite will happen—peace and avoidance or resolution of conflict. During times of stress and anxiety, instead of trying to defend yourself, try staying silent and just listening to the person who is being critical or complaining about you or even calling you names. You will see that your silence will deescalate tension and lead to an opportunity to change the usual practice of fighting fire with fire, which almost always leads to flames for all. When tensions arise in others who start to blame, stay calm and respectful, waiting for a time when tensions are not as high to address the conflict.

Find Areas of Agreement

I recently heard a TED Talk given by a debate champion. She said that the secret to winning and disarming your opponent is by verbally agreeing with some aspect of their argument. That throws off the opponent, causing them to lose their train of thought, which often ends with them stumbling during a debate. The point is to try, if at all possible, to avoid conflict, particularly with family and friends who are part of your support system. Instead, do not be quick to defend yourself; listen attentively with an attitude of wanting to learn and understand. Do all you can to secure peace and harmony in your home because that is your refuge.

Of course, I acknowledge that there are some people who are so negative, bitter, and angry that it is now part of their personality. Such people always seem to be angry with life and with others. No one seems to influence them positively. Being with such a person can indeed be toxic. Try to avoid these individuals if you can. I recognize that some may be relatives; therefore, you cannot be free from them. If you cannot avoid them, seek professional help, such as from a therapist, to make decisions on how to interact with such people.

MY OWN NOTES AND REFLECTIONS ON CHAPTER 24

Questions and activities to consider, besides your own notes.

Describe your family and interpersonal relationship with those in your current household and with your family of origin (i.e., parents or guardians) in terms of how supportive you all are toward one another and also the areas of conflict. Which relationships are at risk of being affected by the stress caused by any crisis, like the pandemic or economic downturns?

Try listening and staying quiet when people are criticizing you or are angry with you. Pay attention to how silence causes tensions to reduce. Also, pay attention to what happens when you surprise angry speakers with some level of agreement. Develop a plan for how to reduce and possibly eliminate tension and conflict. Make sure to have a timeline associated with the plan. Feel free to include contacting agencies that can help you in your plan.

_____

_____

_____

_____

_____

_____

_____

_____

_____

_____

_____

_____

_____

_____

_____

_____

_____

CHAPTER 25

SCAPEGOATING, BLAMING, AND LYING

N o one wants to feel like a failure or admit that they are wrong. From a young age, we learned to try to avoid blame at all cost. For example, let's say that a mother of two six-year-old twin daughters comes home to see muddy footprints on her previously clean floor. She might call out, "Who the heck walked in with mud on their shoes?!" Both daughters had been walking in and out of the home, but the one who had more mud on her shoes is conveniently blamed by the sister with less mud. Everyone, both young and old, has a natural tendency to protect their image and avoid blame. We avoid blame because we do not want to disappoint people who are important to us, like our parents. Unfortunately, those patterns that were formed when we were young stay with us as adults, and we continue to look for ways to avoid blame by placing it on others. Learning to take the blame instead of deflecting it on others is an important life skill that must be practiced.

Accept Responsibility

I do not mean that we have to always assume responsibility and blame blindly. However, avoid blaming others when you find that you have financial problems, are unable to make payments, are short in cash, or do not know what decision to make. Instead of blaming others, get into the habit of encouraging or motivating others. Be willing to listen closely and to accept responsibility when you should. Accepting responsibility does not make you a bad person. We too often use labels when we blame (e.g., "You are such a loser!" "You are so irresponsible!"). Such name calling only increases division and leads to fights. No one can be reduced to a label. We are all irresponsible at times, but it does not mean that we are incorrigible.

Avoid Alienating Others

Communication experts all strongly discourage name calling and suggest that we instead ask those complaining to say what they feel without name calling. Also, avoid using phrases like "You always ..." or "You never ..." Doing so simply labels people and puts them in a box. For example, suppose you told a friend about a promising job opportunity and then found out that they didn't apply. You might be tempted to say something like "You never listen to me. You are so lazy and irresponsible." A better alternative is using "I feel" phrases, such as "I feel like you could have applied for the job but chose not to, which makes me feel like you don't appreciate my friendship." Note that the person saying this avoids name calling and simply conveys what they are feeling and indicating why they are upset.

Learn About Effective Communication

Read articles or books on communication. You will learn the importance of listening to others and of using reflective listening to capture messages and meanings. To return to our previous example, a response that would demonstrate reflective listening would be "I understand that you are telling me that you are upset that I did not apply for the job that you told me I should have. Right?" Such reflective listening validates the person you are communicating with and ensures you understand what they are trying to communicate. The most important thing is for you to not be reactive; instead, pause, listen, and try to understand what others are trying to say. Doing so will convey the importance you place on others. Try to avoid the trap of blaming others to make you feel better. Society, unfortunately, all too often blames others. For instance, many people try to blame immigrants for economic woes, but any economist will tell you that immigrants are never the problem but rather the solution to economic concerns.

Lying

Scapegoating and blaming others leads us into a pattern of not looking at ourselves objectively and leads us to conflict since we can impulsively shift the focus to someone else. The tendency to scapegoat and blame others is related to another problem we sometimes have, lying. I have some relatives who find it so easy to lie. They have developed such creative ways of justifying lying. They might say "I didn't want to hurt their feelings" or "Why tell them the truth if it will only hurt them." This is a form of conflict avoidance, lying to evade the discomfort of having to justify or explain things. The problem is that the habit of lying always leads to mistrust because lies are usually obvious. A relative who was visiting us from out of town said that she needed to leave the family gathering early because she needed to get a part for her mother's hot tub. Yeah, right. On Thanksgiving Day?? I don't think so. It was obvious that she had some gathering she was going to, perhaps with friends or a prospective boyfriend. Of course, I did not argue, but knowing that she lied made it clear she lies, and that knowledge leads to mistrust, creating a wedge between us that doesn't need to be there.

This chapter focuses on a common problem that people have with scapegoating, blaming, and lying. We all have the tendency to do these things. However, some people tend to give into this inclination more than others. The stress we have when we are going through a hard time finding professional employment or earning enough money sometimes cause us to blame others, scapegoat, and lie. This happens almost impulsively, in an attempt to protect ourselves. However, as discussed, this leads to conflict and mistrust that cause us to have even more stress and anxiety because we are losing the support we need of people in our social support system. Understanding the consequences of doing so and seeing the benefit of telling the truth and of accepting blame will allow us to develop and maintain trusting relationships. We need to learn how to communicate with one another truthfully without alienating others. This requires us to learn what effective communication is.

MY OWN NOTES AND REFLECTIONS
ON CHAPTER 25

Describe your household in terms of being at risk for blaming or scapegoating due to the challenges caused by the pandemic or recession. What are the areas of greatest need in your household related to interpersonal blaming and scapegoating?

Sit down with those in your household and talk about how the current crises make it tempting to blame or scapegoat and agree to not do so. Talk about the consequences of blaming others, which include adding to household tension, mistrust, developing hurtful feelings, and so on. Jointly develop a strategy for avoiding blaming and scapegoating that starts with avoiding for at least seven days saying "You this or that ..." or beginning sentences with "You always ..." "You are ..." or "Why can't you ..." and avoiding any other common phrases that imply you are blaming others. Discuss with those near you the consequences of lying and the importance of not doing so.

CHAPTER 26

YOUR HOME AS A SAFE HAVEN

H ome is where you are supposed to feel safe, secure, appreciated, and valued. Alternatively, home can also be a place that is constantly tense and where people are constantly criticized, devalued, and made to feel unsafe. As a society, we place so much value and importance on the concept of home. For some, home can go quickly from a positive environment to a negative environment—one to avoid. As you know, even in "normal" families or households, environments can change very quickly. For many of you, your home is one made up of roommates. If so, you may have two homes—one where you live and one where your family of origin is. In theory, you can have two different home environments, one positive and another negative. Personally, I love my home and marriage. I often feel so lucky to be married to my wife because I feel so secure with her and feel free to be myself. I have nothing to hide from her and vice versa. However, there are times when we do not see eye to eye, and each of us blames the other for not understanding things the way we see them. In those moments, it is so clear to me who is at fault and the same goes for her—of course, it is always the other person. When that happens, I feel angry, or even betrayed, because I feel so certain that I am not to blame. This is why it is sometimes so difficult to resolve a fight, because neither one of us feels we are to blame.

You will notice that family or intimate-partner fights and conflicts tend to happen when we are most stressed and anxious. During the pandemic, graduation ceremonies are done virtually or are being cancelled, we are having to stay isolated at home for long periods of time, and some are losing jobs and income or, for those still in school, you might be doing poorly on exams or assignments. All these experiences increase our internal tension, stress, and anxiety. Imagine if the other members of our intimate circle have similar challenges and concerns. They too will be tense and anxious. That is a perfect recipe for interpersonal conflict. First and foremost, you need to know that stress and anxiety caused by external factors will increase the chances of evoking conflict. Knowing this fact should make it easier to pause and not play into our tendency to get angry and blame others. This does not mean that you should ignore and overlook challenges that cause stress, which could lead to those bottled up emotions exploding into a conflict. Instead, talk about them with your intimate circle of supporters. Openly discuss personal tendencies to scapegoat, get angry, and blame others, as mentioned in the previous chapter. Acknowledge that this is a normal human inclination and tendency. Learn to talk openly about problems facing you in the various realms of work, finances, school, and with interpersonal relationships. Here is an example of a statement that acknowledges conflict but does so in a way that avoids placing blame: "This situation is very challenging for me and it is messing with my emotions and sense of security! And perhaps it is this way for the both of us!"

Next, consider the issues that are making you angry, frustrated, or resentful and minimize them consciously. Sometimes, it is something little that becomes big such as your partner burning dinner or forgetting to get something at the store ("You burnt the dinner!!" or "We don't have any more hamburger meat!!"). Stop, think, and consider for a moment. For the sake of peace and tranquility, say to yourself, "So what? It really is not important!" or "We can eat something else!" Let it go and do not look back. I promise you that you will be happier if you let it go. When we are stressed and anxious, we also say things that we do not mean. People in our intimate circle have a lot of ammunition they can use to upset us because they know us well and know our weaknesses and sensitivities. They can at any point touch the most sensitive part of us. Perhaps they are aware that you are self-conscious about a recent weight gain. In a moment of anger, they might say, "You're eating too much and getting fatter!" Some comments are plain mean and uncalled for, and you may feel justified to defend yourself and say even meaner things back—resist this urge! As mentioned earlier in the book, silence is probably the most powerful tool you have to make people think and regret what they said. It is okay to feel hurt, but do not make things worse by expanding the conflict. You know that the person is simply angry and does not really mean what they said and will regret it later. Plan to discuss it later, and perhaps convey it in writing in a note that you can discuss together when you have time and are not as stressed.

To avoid being in a stressful and toxic environment, you need to see yourself as a peacemaker who actively works toward making your home environment tranquil, safe, and enjoyable. I realize that for some people, living in a state of conflict is normal. I have family members where that is the case. They cannot seem to avoid fighting. The way they talk to each other sets them up for conflict. The blaming voice, the quick reaction to what is being said, and the immediate skepticism and criticism is always on the tip of their tongue. The strange thing is that sometimes they are the nicest people outside of their intimate circle of family members. Such families that have deep-rooted tendencies to engage in conflict have to unlearn dysfunctional patterns of communication. They can learn to break these patterns on their own, but the quickest way to change is to seek help from therapists who specialize in communication and family dynamics or couple's therapy.

The point of this chapter is to emphasize that we all have the ability to contribute to peace and create a safe home environment. Everyone has a choice and the power to influence their environments one way or another. If members of an intimate circle cannot hold back from negativity, then professional help should be sought to learn ways of interacting with such members.

MY OWN NOTES AND REFLECTIONS
ON CHAPTER 26

Questions and activities to consider, besides your own notes.

Is your household a safe haven? To what extent do members of your household talk about negative things that are happening outside of the home, like job losses or reduced income? Develop a daily schedule for members of the household to take time to talk about stress, anxiety, fears, and sadness or depression to develop a plan for making sure that such feelings are heard and not allowed to lead to interpersonal conflict.

_____

_____

_____

_____

_____

_____

_____

_____

_____

_____

_____

_____

_____

_____

_____

_____

_____

_____

_____

_____

_____

_____

CHAPTER 27

BE AT PEACE WITH OTHERS AND WITH THE WORLD

W e are currently living through one of the most polarizing periods in American history. For example, we have the pandemic crisis, concern regarding police brutality, and until recently, political polarization. The last time we were so divided was during the Civil War when the South was fighting the North to maintain its economic system that relied on slave labor. It can be argued that the Civil War was in part the consequence of the United States' massive growth in population and economy during the 19th century. A big part of its growth hinged on its diverse immigrant population. From 1850 to 1900, the United States increased its population by over 150%, going from 23 million to 76 million people, most being newly arrived immigrants.[1] Therefore, the character of the nation was changing as was its economy, which was increasingly becoming mechanized as a result of the Industrial Revolution of that period. We needed that growth in population if we were to become a world economic leader with a rich economy. Immigrants, like the Irish, Polish, and Italians, were initially discriminated against violently, but eventually, many of these immigrants became integrated. As of this writing, the United States has a population of over 332 million people. The economy over the past 50 years has gone through a major change, with the United States, along with all other countries, becoming more globalized due to accessible transportation and communication. Very few complex products being manufactured, such as computers and cars, have parts that are from only one country anymore.

Our economy over the past 50 years has gone from being a largely domestic economy to one that is global. As such, many large companies are no longer rooted in one country. Instead, a company or corporation will have its beginning history rooted in one region of the country or state, and within a few years, and sometimes suddenly, decide to move to another state or even another country in search of larger profit margins. That is now the norm in our globalized economy, and we need to accept it. Without strong pro-worker government policies requiring greater company and corporate or organizational commitments and loyalty toward their workforce, workers will continue to feel vulnerable, burdened with an unstable income and with an inherent inability to plan for their long-term future. The current corporate focus on bottom line profits for owners or stockholders will only lead to continued increases in workforce insecurity, fear, anxiety, and mistrust by others, especially immigrants or those most discriminated against, including women. It is important not to fall into political rhetoric that puts blame on specific populations or groups, because they are not the problem; instead, it is the world economy and the effects of globalization, which are here to stay.

The negative side of globalization and economic change is the lack of stability that the workforce experiences. The positive side of it is the ever-evolving opportunities globalization offers to those going into professional fields. The current pandemic crisis is, for example, changing the way we teach and use technology for instruction and learning. New professional jobs are emerging to fill this niche of technology and learning. Similarly, health care is also changing. Tasks that used to be the responsibility of nurses are now being given to a number of emerging medical assistant careers and licensed positions or occupations. Labor statistics suggest that the typical American worker stays in their jobs for an average of about 4.4 years.[2] If most adults work an average of 40 years in their lifetime, then current workers are likely to work in an average of 14 jobs or more in their lifetime. That means that current college graduates will need to be prepared for change and for seeking new opportunities. Their job-seeking skills and career skill set will need to be continually evolving and improving. This can be seen a scary and challenging situation or as positive and exciting one. Our perspective, how we see things, is critical. A positive perspective helps develop and maintain an optimistic outlook that helps you succeed since having the opposite will only cause you to spiral into sadness, depression, and anxiety.

Nurture a Positive Outlook and Perspective

To develop and maintain a positive perspective, you need to have valid reasons for being happy and positive. Just as there are a million reasons that the world offers us every day for why we should be sad, angry, anxious, and negative, there are an equal, if not, greater number of reasons to be positive and optimistic. Looking at others in a positive light is so vitally important. As mentioned earlier in the book, when we are stressed, we have a tendency to blame others. This is destructive and only leads to negativity dwelling inside us. Instead, we need to be positive and optimistic toward our life and the world. Think of valid reasons to be optimistic and positive. To begin, consider that we are alive and breathing. We may be able to add the ability to walk, smell, taste, see, hear, and think to that list. These are just the very basics. I am sure that if you try, you can fill in the rest of the reasons to be happy and positive. These are sometimes called gratitude lists, and they are a great tool to use for remaining positive. The fact is that we can choose to focus on the positives or the negatives—it is a personal choice that has immediate and lasting consequences.

Therefore, a big part of being positive is the choice we make to focus on valid reasons for feeling and thinking this way. Another contributor to that choice is who we hang out with. Choosing to be around those who are positive, joyous, optimist and cheerful will most definitely influence us, our mood, and our outlook. What we watch on television or read on social media or news outlets will also influence our outlook. Here is a list of twelve ways to stay positive and happy I have developed with help from an online article on the subject:

1. **Make an effort to find a positive side in everything**—as mentioned earlier, it is your choice.

2. **Be grateful**—appreciate everything that you have and have around you, including who you are.

3. **Create a positive environment**—be around people who are positive; consume media that is positive.

4. **Exercise more**—do at least 20 minutes of exercise a day; it will lead to increases in endorphins that affect your mood, health, and well-being.

5. **Treasure your experiences more than possessions**—become less materialistic and assign more value to experiences with people, including those pleasant ones experienced in the past.

6. **Help others**—you always feel better when giving or helping others, which leads to an appreciation of others, gratitude, unity, and internal peace.

7. **Go outdoors**—being in fresh air and seeing the beauty in vegetation around us leads to enhanced mood and excitement.

8. **Meditation**—including mindfulness, can help you calm down and focus on what is important.

9. **Get enough sleep**—getting at least 7 to 8 hours of sleep allows us to have control over our emotions and helps us to stay healthy.

10. **Express your feelings**—more than the effect of catharsis, having a social support system with close confidants to share thoughts and experiences helps us to feel hopeful and happy.

11. **Reduce your worries**—worries will always be there; actively work toward not allowing them to dominate your thinking and emotions.

12. **Accept and find solutions**—be adaptable and accepting of change even if you did not choose it and convert change into a positive experience.[3]

I would also add to the list the importance of a healthy diet—minimize intake of sugars, processed food, and carbs and restrict alcohol use during your most stressful times. Sugars, carbs (converts into sugars), and alcohol always give you an immediate high followed by a just as immediate low as your body pumps out great amounts of insulin. While it is not much acknowledged, research shows that drinking even moderate amounts of alcohol increases stress, anxiety, and depression the following day. Actively put to practice these 12 steps and advice, paying particular attention to the benefits of exercising, eating well, and minimizing your intake of alcohol and other substances that can develop into addictions. I know we discussed these factors earlier, but I believe they are worth reiterating here.

Limit Your Dose of Bad News

Television, radio, and the internet are now replete with negative and fearful news. Until recently, we had political divisions that polarized the country. We also have had protests over systemic racism and police brutality (e.g., police officers killing George Floyd). Regarding the pandemic crisis, we still lack a lot of information about the SARS-CoV-2 virus and its variants that causes COVID-19. This uncertainty leads to stress and anxiety, with people wondering: "How many breaths of exhumed aerosol air or number of droplets from an infected person does it take for us to get infected when breathing? How easy is it to contact the virus from various surfaces touched by infected individuals? How do I know that I will not be among the atypical young people who die from the virus if infected? Should I get vaccinated? Is it safe to do so? Will vaccination really protect me? Also, will I be able to find a professional job with my degree given that there is a growing number of unemployed? How will I pay my rent and bills?" This is why the media is so important; it keeps us informed. It is the nonstop, large doses of bad news and the focus on sensationalism that cause us to be anxious and to lose hope. You have to actively limit the amount of news you consume and pay attention to the source, separating those that thrive on sensationalism and exaggeration from those that provide unbiased information based on facts. To do so, start by asking yourself what types of news stories are essential and what are their purpose. Here are examples of some types of news stories that can be relevant and beneficial:

Policies and Laws: Keeps us informed of government policies and laws that guide or limit our behavior. For example, knowing if parks are open now to the public, enforcement of wearing face masks, and so on.

- **Updates on Important Issues Dear to Us:** You may have particular issues that are important for you personally and that you want to know how they are evolving. For example, I may be interested in working with people who are homeless. In that case, knowing about how a recession and pandemic are affecting people who are homeless would be important for me.
- **Entertainment:** Information can provide us with entertaining possibilities, such as knowing what sports team is likely to win a championship or learning new recipes that we want to try.
- **Engendering Hope:** News can give us hope about when this pandemic crisis will be behind us or how vaccine roll-out could sooner get ourselves and loved ones closer to total inoculation against the pandemic virus.
- **Inspirational and Spiritual:** News can be inspirational when we learn of people who risked their lives when saving the life of another or when they share their resources. It can also feed our spiritual self, like when we read of how people's faith kept them psychologically secure or helped them continue with their life goal or pursuits.
- **Informing of Opportunities:** New stories can inform us of the growth in jobs in certain sectors, such as recent announcements by Amazon calling for the hiring of warehouse workers and delivery drivers.

Use this list to decide what your news priorities are and write out a plan for how much news you will consume and from what sources you will get it. Limit the amount of time you spend catching up on news. Also, limit your time spent on social media—which can be a source of unreliable and sensational news. Start and end each day with positive information and keep negative news to just the middle of the day when it does not risk permeating the day.

Read Biographies

Regardless of the medium, be it listening to a lecture, podcast, or audiobook or physically reading a book, we always learn new things that impact our lives when we know of past people's life experiences, their struggles and achievements, and how they handled stress and overcame adversity. If you do not know which career to pursue, read biographies of those that were also unsure but ended up finding their focus. If you wish to become a nurse or educator or speech and language pathologist, read biographies of those who ended up choosing those fields. Reading is best, but as an alternative, you can view films or television programs that depict the life of people with whom you can identify.

Develop Your Spiritual Self to Rest and Enhance Hope

According to the National Alliance on Mental Health, religion and spirituality help to provide answers to profound questions that we all have as human beings.[4] They can provide answers to such question as "What is the meaning of life?" and "What is my purpose here on this earth?" They can teach us the value of others and the importance of forgiveness—both giving and receiving it. They can also give you an immediate social support system rooted in a particular religious or spiritual community. You can feel connected to others and therefore not feel alone. They can also provide you with a sense of hope. For example, I love reading the book of Psalms in the Bible written by King David because each psalm is so human-centered, reflecting the presence of doubts, anger, and frustrations while also having hope in God—a power that is greater than us or greater than those forces that you fear or have no control over. Religion and spirituality can also teach us concern and compassion toward others in need. Once when living in Kansas City, I remember seeing the cloudy sky turn into an eerie greenish haze. There was a tornado warning, and all of a sudden, it started to hail stones of ice as big as baseballs. The lightning was relentless, one strike after the other, coming down within a five-mile radius of me. At that moment, it did not matter that I lived in a powerful and prosperous country, that I was an educated and esteemed individual, or that I had a loving family to protect. I and others around me were so small and puny compared to the powerful sky around me. That, to me, is also spiritual in that it puts human beings in our place. We may think we are the be-all and end-all, but we are not. Whether or not you consider yourself religious, whether or not you believe in a God or higher power, I suggest you get into the habit of practicing meditation and mindfulness, which will help you appreciate who you are and what you have as you seek guidance, forgiveness, and help. Call it part of meditation or quiet time. If you make this a routine, you will find that you will feel more at peace and have a more positive outlook toward life and your future.

This chapter covers things we should do in order to be at peace with the world and with others. Being at peace with others is a decision we have control over. There are things we can choose that will affect our mental state, which include who we surround ourselves with and what media we consume. It also includes what we eat and how we take care of our bodies by eating well and not ingesting harmful substances. Beyond that, we can also decide to learn from others and how they made wise choices and overcame obstacles in their lives. Finally, we can mediate and practice mindfulness where we focus on appreciating who we are and the resources we have regardless of the struggles we may have, including finding employment. We need to acknowledge that we not only have a lot of control over our emotions but also over our fate.

Notes

1. Demographic history of the United States. (2020). In *Wikipedia*. Last modified version on April 9, 2020. https://en.wikipedia.org/wiki/Demographic_history_of_the_United_States
2. Meister, J. (2012). The future of work: Job hopping is the "new normal" for millennials. *Forbes*. https://www.forbes.com/sites/jeannemeister/2012/08/14/the-future-of-work-job-hopping-is-the-new-normal-for-millennials/#40c4f23113b8
3. Angela, L. (2019). *12 simple ways to stay positive and happy: Shifting perspective can help you live a happier, more fulfilling life*. Thrive Global. https://thriveglobal.com/stories/12-simple-ways-to-stay-positive-and-happy/
4. Greenstein, L. (2016). The mental health benefits of religion and spirituality. *National Alliance on Mental Health* (NAMI blog). https://www.nami.org/Blogs/NAMI-Blog/December-2016/The-Mental-Health-Benefits-of-Religion-Spiritual

MY OWN NOTES AND REFLECTIONS
ON CHAPTER 27

Develop a plan for making sure you and those you live with maintain a peaceful home environment even while being overwhelmed by all that is going on in society.

How will you limit the bad news you receive yet stay informed? What positive sources of information will you seek out to encourage you and provide you with a positive outlook toward your future? What things can you do to improve your physical health and well-being? To what extent do you have a spiritual side that offers you comfort and answers to life's questions? Dedicate yourself to a practice of meditation or mindfulness that will help you appreciate life and give you a sense of tranquility.

_____

_____

_____

_____

_____

_____

_____

_____

_____

_____

_____

_____

_____

_____

_____

_____

_____

_____

_____

_____

YOUR PERSONAL NOTES

I recognize that this book, being a *survival manual*, does not cover every topic or encompass all that can be helpful to you. It admittedly has a lot of subjective advice based on my own experience as a research psychologist and as a professor who has been teaching university students for many years. There are bound to be omissions and necessary corrections or updates. Use these next few blank pages to fill in the gaps and to jot your notes and reactions to what is suggested to you in the *manual*. There is blank space purposely left at the end of each chapter for you to react to each topic, to add to the discussion, help you plan, and give advice to yourself. Feel free to also email me what you think are the gaps or needed updates that I should include in the book for me to consider in future editions. After all, you are the audience that I am interested in helping, and therefore, you are the ultimate experts on what your needs are. I recognize that you also have a lot of helpful advice to share, which can be included in future editions. I look forward to hearing from you and of knowing whether this book was of help to you.

Your Personal Notes and Additions to This Manual

Write any notes and plans for your professional journey that this *survival manual* helped you with or that prompted you to think about. *What areas were not covered in the manual that you wished it had covered? What are those areas mentioned in the manual that you will use to either develop plans for or take steps in for your benefit? To what extent do you feel more positive about your degree and what you can do with it? Develop a plan of action or steps you will take to start your professional career.*

_____

_____

CPSIA information can be obtained
at www.ICGtesting.com
Printed in the USA
BVHW011456310122
627619BV00005B/38